Positive Puppy T for Beginners

The Complete Step by Step Practical Guide to Raising a Happy and Amazing Dog Using the Power of Positive Reinforcement

By
Matthew Hargreaves

Table of Contents

Introduction

So, you've just got a new puppy. You're ecstatic because it's cute and it's going to grow up to be a good boy/girl. Well, they will not be well behaved if you do not train him/her properly. We all want our dogs to be well-behaved so you know they won't cause any trouble when you take them anywhere. You don't want a puppy that you cannot control and just relieves itself everywhere, right?

This is where this book comes in. I am going to give you practical advice on how you can train your own puppy right at home. We will go over how to take your four-legged friend from being completely wild to a well-behaved puppy in less than a month! If you are one of those owners who are frustrated with their own pups not listening to their commands, then this book is perfect for you. I will show you how you can put an end to such behavior immediately.

My name is Matthew Hargreaves and I have been working with these good boys for several years. I have trained so many dogs from different breeds and sizes that I've lost count. It is true that training dogs is a lot different to working in the office, but it is something that I am very passionate about. My parents were also avid dog lovers and we have had dogs in our home since I can remember. Four of my most favorite pups Rex (Corgi), Snow (Husky), Ginger (Border Collie), and Mutt (Bulldog) inspired me to follow this career path. After learning that my neighbor treated their dogs rather poorly, I have decided to write this book. I want to show everyone that, with a little bit of training, dogs really are a man's best friend.

I have seen many problematic dogs that people have brought to me. In the end, I change those troubled pups into the lovable canine friends that we all used to know and adore. People thank me for my work and how my training has changed their life. Through my training, those dog owners can start to build a deep and meaningful relationship with their dog. It thrills me to no end to see how my work has influenced people's lives. This also happens to be a reason why I have written this book. I want both dogs and humans to live in harmony by helping the latter understand dog psychology. I will unveil the exact same training I used on dogs in this book. I'm talking about the kind of training that is easy to follow and get quick results. It does not have to be hard, expensive, or stressful for both animals and humans.

With my expertise, you will be fully equipped with the skills and knowledge you need to train your puppy. It will go from being a naughty little troublemaker to an obedient, friendly, and loyal dog.

Have you ever heard the saying, "Old habits die hard", or "You can't teach an old dog new tricks"? It is true, both for animals and humans. The best time for your dog to learn is when it is young. Think of your pup's brain like a sponge. As your dog grows up, it will pick up certain behaviors and habits, which will fill up the sponge. Eventually, your dog will find it hard to learn new habits or tricks. Therefore, it is crucial to train your puppy as early and as young as possible, or you will miss out on the most valuable and effective time to train your dog. As I said, I have worked with many dogs and from my personal experience, training puppies is much easier compared to older dogs. So, do not wait around to train your puppy.

The puppy training tips and tricks I will show you in this book are proven to be effective and offer incredible results for puppies of all ages, breeds, and sizes. Every chapter in this book will provide you with valuable insights into the mind of your canine companion as well as actionable steps to help you curb your puppies' undesirable habits and behavior, as well as instill good values and dog qualities. That way, you can take your dog anywhere without worries. If you follow my instructions in this book closely, it is very likely that you may never have to train your dog ever again.

Chapter 1: Why Positive Training is Perfect for Your Dog

While there are many ways to train a puppy, five of the most commonly used types of training are:

Alpha Dog or Dominance

This training method is popularized by Cesar Millan. However, he also combines dominance training with other forms of training when needed. It uses the dog's pack mentality to establish a relationship of dominance and submission. You see, dogs see humans as a part of their own pack and they have a social hierarchy similar to that of wolves. When a dog sees itself as the alpha, it becomes disobedient. Because you are considered to be a part of the pack, you need to show dominance and teach your dog to respect you as the alpha in the pack and submit.

However, showing dominance does not involve violence. You need to understand the dog's body language and learn how to respond properly. That way, you can project authority and confidence. This includes eating before the dog, enter or leaving the room before your dog, and taking it for walks on a leash. Your dog needs to sit and wait at the door if it wants to be let outside. It needs to wait while you prepare food. With this kind of training, you need to be careful with your behavior as well. That means you do not allow the dog to be on the couch or bed with you. You do not lean down to your dog's eye level. Doing so tells your dog that it is equal to you. That is the opposite of what you are trying to achieve with this training. You need to show your dog that you are dominant and in charge.

Does it sound strict? Yes, but it is for your dog's own good. You teach it how to be disciplined. However, this type of training is becoming less and less popular. Some modern trainers have stopped using this technique as they consider it to be outdated. This belief is further reinforced when research has shown that the pack dynamics observed in wolves is not the same to dogs due to the difference in the wild and captivity. Of course, dominance training can be a quick way to curb unwanted behavior, but it might fail to address the underlying causes of your dog's bad behavior. This can leave your dog feeling anxious or fearful, which is not a healthy relationship you want to have with your beloved pet. Plus, this type of training can create a dominance struggle which can be constant and require consistent reinforcement. Not only the fact this is tedious and difficult, but it can also be dangerous for children or elderly.

Electronic Training

Electronic training uses an electronic collar that either shocks the dog or sprays it with citronella whenever the dog fails to perform the desired task. It is mainly used at a distance when a leash cannot be used.

For instance, you may see such training methods being used on dogs to teach them to remain within a certain area in an unfenced yard. It can also be used to teach dogs to work in the field or hunt.

While people who use electronic collars say that this type of training has less risk of dog injury compared to a choke collar or other mechanical devices, there are many issues with this training method. You see, the device only punishes the dog so it knows what it is not supposed to do. This does not necessarily mean that it knows what it should do. Moreover, it creates a lot of stress for the poor animal and may cause it to develop permanent anxiety.

You may see this device being used by professional trainers. They may get the desired result from this type of training. However, the electronic collar is often used by inexperienced owners who tend to overuse it. This can cause their pets to experience unnecessary pain, both psychologically and physically. It is obvious that this kind of training is not supposed to be used by average owners. Thankfully, there are many other ways to train dogs without subjecting it to so much stress and pain.

If you do wish to use one, consult a professional so you at least know how to use it properly. Still, I urge you to consider an alternative form of behavior correction methods.

Scientific Training

This type of training seeks to understand dogs' nature and use it to teach them certain behaviors based on their ability to be conditioned, as well as understanding the effectiveness of rewards and punishments to dogs. However, it is hard to define because it relies on practices and information that are believed to be the most accurate at its time. That means it will change in the future as new discoveries are being made.

Animal behaviorists are continually expanding our understanding of dog psychology with new studies and experiments. They are vital as trainers rely on these studies in order to work with dogs effectively. It makes sense that we need to understand a behavior first before we attempt to change it.

Since this training is so broad, it is difficult to say exactly what the overarching methodology is behind it. In reality, many methods in other types of training are based on scientific training. Most of the time, we rely on operant conditioning that includes positive reinforcements and, in rare cases, certain forms of punishment. Certain scientific trainers believe that we should try to find out how to reinforce good behaviors in puppies without the use of rewards and use dog psychology to improve off-leash relationships between the puppies and their owners.

What we know is that we can rely on this kind of training as it is based on a large amount of research. You also need to stay up to date on the latest studies. This can be tedious, so it may be better to leave the scientific stuff for the professional trainers because the methods they use are effective most of the time, whether you understand the science behind it or not. Plus, many other methods of training are based on scientific training anyway.

Still, we advise against developing new forms of training based on one study alone. It takes a lot of research and experimenting before one can discover a new training method. Again, leave it to the professionals. However, it is a good idea to stay informed and pay attention to new studies when it becomes available. The insights they provide may be useful to help you train your pup.

Clicker training

Clicker training is based on operant conditioning that we mentioned previously. It also relies heavily on the principles in positive reinforcement, which we will get to in a moment. In reality, you can put clicker training under the positive reinforcement umbrella. This training method uses a device that makes a quick, sharp noise such as a whistle or a clicker to tell the dog when it has accomplished a desired behavior.

The upside of clicker training is that it tells your pup exactly when it has accomplished a wanted behavior and it knows what is being rewarded. You can use the clicker to easily teach puppies new behaviors in addition to adding verbal commands.

It works like this; First, your pup needs to be conditioned to know that a click means that a reward is coming. Then, you can train your dog so it knows how to associate a certain behavior to the click and the reward. Finally, you can add a verbal command so you can introduce a new form of association.

This type of training is effective when you try to teach your pooch new tricks, not much so when you need to curb its unwanted behaviors. You can even use it to train your pup to perform complicated tasks. Many professional trainers also use clicker training. When you combine this training method with others, it can be an effective way to train your puppy.

A word of warning, though. Some people have reported issues with these training methods. While it is one of the easiest methods of dog training in the short term, it may be counterproductive in the long run. The problem is that your dog may become conditioned to the click and will not obey commands without it. Moreover, you need to have excellent timing skills. A split second delay in your click can result in the wrong action being registered, which may confuse your dog.

Positive Reinforcement

We will focus on positive reinforcement in this book because I believe this is the best training method. This training method is popularized by trainers such as Dawn Sylvia-Stasiewicz who trained Bo, Obama's dog. The idea behind it is pretty simple. Dogs will repeat good behavior when you give it rewards. The form of punishment is the lack of rewards. So, if your dog is being naughty, it gets nothing. That way, it knows when it gets something right and when it has done something wrong. You can step up the punishment further by taking its treats or toys away. Such form of punishment does not involve physical punishment, so your dogs do not become permanently anxious or hurt emotionally or physically.

Just like clicker training, this training method starts by rewarding your pup when it has accomplished the desired behavior immediately (or within seconds) after it happens. That way, your dog associates that behavior with the reward so it is encouraged to repeat such behavior again for the reward. Some professional trainers use this alongside clicker training that we talked about. This kind of training tells your pup exactly when it has completed the desired behavior. You can improve its effectiveness by using short commands such as sit, stay, and come.

Positive reinforcement requires consistency. That means that everyone in your home needs to use the same commands and follow the same reward system for this kind of training to be effective. First, start by rewarding your puppy continuously whenever it does the right thing. Then, you can start to give it rewards less frequently as you observe that the behavior starts to become a habit – that is when it isn't done for the sake of rewards anymore. In some cases, beginner trainers may accidentally reward bad behavior such as letting the dog out when it barks at a squirrel or another dog. Simply correct this erroneous behavior by stopping giving your dog rewards, and it should change eventually.

Rewards do not just have to be treats. You can also use toys, praises, or pets as rewards, and you should because it can be easy to overfeed your pooch when it is learning. I suggest you use small treats in the early stage, then move to toys, praises, then pets as rewards as the behavior becomes more natural.

Again, this kind of training is best used to teach puppies new behaviors, but not so effective if you try to curb unwanted behaviors. Still, all it takes is patience.

While all the methods I described above work, I believe that the best method to train your puppies is positive reinforcement. Not only that it is effective, but it is also simple so even first-time puppy owners can teach their pups how to behave properly without the risk of hurting their lovely pets. Of course, not all dogs are created equal (although they all are good boys/girls). So, your puppy may respond differently from other dogs under the same training method. Even so, positive reinforcement is well-received by many puppies.

Dog's Behavior

If you wish to train your dog, you need to understand the way they think and act first.

Communication

We talk to each other using our voice, although many of us can understand each other more if we observe each other's body language. Dogs, on the other hand, primarily talk to each other through eye gaze, facial expression, body posture, gustatory communication (taste, scents, etc.) or vocalization. Vocalization is hardly used among dogs other than growls, bark, and whines. Most of the talking between dogs is body language.

Many of us communicate with dogs through vocalization, but you can see how inefficient it is. Dogs can learn to understand our emotions based on our facial expressions, but it is better if we use body language as a primary medium of communication because dogs can understand that a lot better.

Social Behavior

Dogs behave differently based on their size. This is why smaller breeds such as the Chihuahua are super aggressive whereas giant breeds such as St. Bernard are gentle and very lovable giants. Manypeer-reviewed studies on dogs identified seven dimensions of canine personality:

- Activity
- Sociability (starting friendly interactions with other dogs or humans)
- Responsiveness to training
- Fearfulness (shaking)
- Submissiveness
- Aggression
- Reactivity (approach or avoidance of strange new objects)

Again, it all depends on the dog's breed as I have mentioned earlier, although age and gender have not been clearly confirmed to play a role in dogs' personality. This personality model can be used to determine if a dog is suitable for a range of tasks, one of which is finding the right family to re-home shelter dogs.

Play

Playtime between dogs normally displays certain behaviors that are often seen in aggressive situations such as growling, nipping, biting, whining or even barking. This is why socialization is important as dogs need to learn these behaviors in the context of play rather than aggression. Biting, for instance, employs much less force when used in play compared to aggression. You may hear a yelp and the bitten pup runs away from the offending puppy. That means the latter bites a little too hard and the play stops then and there because the former thought the bite was an act of aggression. Through trials and errors, they will come around to learn bite inhibition, which is to say that they learn to bite gently.

Play is initiated when dogs show their intent to play by displaying a wide range of behavior such as a "play-bow" in which the dog lays down on its front paws and wags its tail, a "face-pawed" in which they lie down (sometimes on their stomach) and wipes their face with its paws, or "open-mouth play face" in which they jump around, wags its tail, and mouths at the other dog or other postures to invite the other dog to come to play. Very cute indeed. The same signal is displayed throughout the play so both dogs understand that it is still a play, not an act of aggression.

Playing among dogs take the form of a mock fight. It is believed that this rough-and-tumble play is common among puppies, and is the most important behavior training for your pup as it grows up. Bite inhibition is learned through these mock fights. These fights do not have to be a perfect balance between dominance and submissive between the pups involved, but winning does give the pup a self-esteem boost.

There is a common misconception that games such as tug-of-war can change a dog's dominance relationship with humans. This is not true at all. In fact, this is how dogs indicate their temperament and relationship with their owner. It is also worth noting that human-dog play does not replace dog-dog play, so make sure your pup gets to play with other pups as often as possible, especially at an early age.

Dominance

Dogs are pack animals. They have a hierarchy inside the pack and the leader is the alpha dog. The alpha is dominant and often at times aggressive. In your household, you should show your dog that you are his leader, the alpha of the pack, so you can teach them commands and behaviors easily. As I mentioned before, dominance training is not the way to train your dog, but you should assert your position early so your puppy understands. Dominance is not absolute, meaning that if your dog suddenly thinks that it owns the place, you can prove them wrong.

If you have more than one dog at home, you can observe their behaviors to determine which one is the dominant dog. Which one eats first or eats the other dog's food? Which one usually wins in a fight or play? Which one barks first or for longer when a stranger approaches the door?

Dominance is not tied to relative weight or size, although the bigger dog is often the alpha because of sheer strength. You may see a smaller dog with the brains beating its larger counterpart in a fight, although that is a rare sight. However, dogs know how to respect older dogs. Puppies will not pick a fight with a larger and older dog and this respect continues into adulthood. When puppies play together, they come to develop different expectations from the interaction about the likely response they get from each other in different situations. When you introduce adult dogs who have never met before, they will be anxious and vigilant, which you can tell by their tense body and sudden movements. They will survey each other to develop these expectations. Depending on the situation, both dogs will know which dog is the dominant one.

Chapter 2: Essential Skills Your Puppy Needs

Before you can even begin to teach your puppy new tricks, we need to go over some of the most essential skills your puppy needs to condition it to understand commands properly. Your dog needs to be in the proper shape, mind, body, and heart. Those are in addition to all the love and affection to keep your puppy emotionally satisfied.

As a dog owner, you need to keep in mind that both humans and dogs have one thing in common: they both have a high sense of emotions – instinctual and intellectual.

Dog's Emotions

Unlike humans, dogs let their impulse take control. They do what they feel like doing. We humans, we can stop and consider the consequences of our action and behave accordingly. That does not mean that we should consider dogs' natural impulse to be the lack of rationality or lack of learning capacity.

Because dogs think and communicate differently from us, we need to learn how to build a proper communication with your pet. We can start by understanding the dog's specific behavior. Every dog owner needs to understand why their dog is behaving a certain way.

Educating the Dog

It is not so far-fetched when people claim that their dog is their "baby". Having a dog is like having a kid. This implies authority over the pup and responsibility to educate and raise the dog.

You, as a dog owner, are the first person to create a proper bond between the dog, its family (or its pack, you), the surrounding community and environment. Therefore, owning a dog makes you a dog trainer to an extent. It is your responsibility to teach the dog the right way to behave and to understand your dogs' needs based on the responses that they give.

There are a few things you need to keep in mind as a dog trainer:

- Consistent: You must not tolerant an inappropriate behavior from your dog, not even once. If it has been a naughty puppy, make sure your dog knows that. Make it clear that you do not accept such behavior.
- Constant: Your dog can only learn so much, so make sure that your command is constant – that is, not changing. If you want your dog to sit, say "Sit" and "Sit" only. Do not use other commands for the same action, as it will confuse your dog and makes training a lot harder than it should. Any change in tone or attitude from you can and will confuse your dog.

- Behavior: If your dog is constantly being troublesome, try to find the reason behind their behavior. There may be something that makes them that way. When you do find it, remove the source. Figure out what you can do about the problem so your dog can be at peace again. It helps both you and your dog.
- Understand basic dog training rules: You need to understand basic dog training principles like prevention (teach your dog basic behavior to prevent problematic ones such as biting), maintenance (maintain the same training regimen), redirection (you may need to put things in order over again), and reward (show your dog that it is making progress by offering it rewards for its good behavior).

Discipline

Discipline is basically the ability of your dog to obey certain rules that you teach them through different techniques such as body language and energy. So, how can you teach your dog discipline?

The best way to do so is, of course, not through punishment, yelling, or hitting the dog. We need to encourage the dog to act a certain way by emphasizing the active elements of the dog, not instilling our authority as the owner. The latter does not teach your dog the value of rules and commands based on their nature, but they understand it based on what you want – your power as the owner.

So, training a dog requires energy and leadership, not a dictatorship. Moreover, any dog owner knows that not all dogs are created the same, so they have unique limitations with regards to learning, energy, and obeying capacities.

You as a dog owner must support your dog in its discovery of its new environment in the human world by balancing its interaction with humans and other animals. You need the right approach and discipline to achieve this. Of course, love and affection go a long way in the dog's learning process. Keeping yourself calm, empathic, and consistent are also crucial for your pup too.

So, before we go on to teach your dog various commands, there are five proven practices you can do to discipline your dog:

- Walk: Try to take your dog out for a walk for at least 30 minutes in the morning every day. Not only will it improve your dog's body and mind, but it also provides a good opportunity for you to strengthen your bond with your pet. If the dog is untrained, just make sure to keep a close watch on it. It is a good idea to take them for walks to places where they cannot cause trouble.
- Mind Training: This is what this book is all about. Give your dog treats or affection to show a reward for positive behaviors.

- Show that you are his leader: Start by going through doors before your dog. Your dog must walk behind you so it can understand that you are its leader. Otherwise, the hierarchy will be messed up and it thinks that it is controlling you.

- Ask your dog to do something: This is for after you have taught your dog some commands. Before giving your pup something to eat, drink, or play, ask them to perform commands such as "Come" or "Sit". Doing so tells them that it needs to earn their treat.

- Avoid giving attention: Okay, this sounds like a bit of a stretch to purposely ignore your dog. But hear me out. If you give your dog too much attention, it will become hyperactive and anxious, which is something that keeps your pup far from being disciplined. You do not have to ignore your pup regularly, though. You can just occasionally not talk, touch, or maintain eye contact with your dog when it asks for attention.

Frequently Asked Questions

Okay, we know that puppies are super adorable and all that. However, they are a big responsibility. Whether you are an amateur puppy owner or a seasoned veteran, you may have some questions when you bring home that adorable four-legged canine. To help you out with your new journey with your adorable pup, I have rounded up ten questions that dog owners have about puppies.

Housebreaking

Just like us, puppies need some time to get used to its new home. Be patient because it won't be fully potty trained in a single day. Every puppy has its own pace, so I don't suggest you push them beyond that. You can speed up the process by crate-training your dog, which we will get into in the next chapter. After it has familiarized itself with its crate, it sees it as a safe haven and will not soil it. As a general rule, your dog can hold it in for as many hours as its age (in months). For example, if it is 6 months old, it can only hold it in for six hours before it leaks and has to go right then and there. If your puppy does have an accident, do not punish them by hitting them or sticking its nose in it. They're already quite guilty for doing it. Just interrupt with an "Oops" or "No" and take it outside so it can go.

The Vet

Ah, the vet. A place where many animals dread of seeing. Many dog owners do not know what to expect at their first veterinary exam. The process is simple. First, the vet will check your puppy's vitals and asks for its health history. It's a good idea to collect a stool sample from your puppy so the vet can check it for evidence for intestinal parasites and get rid of them if there's any. Then, the vet will check your pup from head to toe for all signs of disease, abnormalities, or other external parasites. If there are any issues, the vet will administer the proper vaccinations depending on your pup's age and vaccination history. Your pup may even get a deworming medication, a flea, and a tick preventive.

The Vaccinations

There are four core vaccines that your puppy needs: rabies, canine distemper, hepatitis (canine adenovirus-2), and canine parvovirus. The rabies vaccination is a one-time administration. Other vaccinations require boosters every three or four weeks. Your vet will discuss the recommended vaccine schedule with you. If you are at the vet, make sure to ask about the optional vaccines for diseases such as kennel cough (bordetella), Lyme disease, leptospirosis, and canine coronavirus.

The Park

You will need to take your dog out to the park eventually. The only problem is when. In the first three months of its life, you should let your dog familiarize itself with the surrounding as much as possible. That means getting it to interact with as many people, places, and experience the world as much as possible. However, just make sure that your pup has got the proper vaccination. It is not a good idea to take your dog to the dog park only to contract a deadly disease such as parvo. Dogs at the park can be ill or unvaccinated and you should not risk it. Wait until you get the go-ahead from your vet.

Training

Another question many dog owners wonder is when can they start training their pup. The answer is as soon as possible. There is no need to wait because training your dog is most effective when it is young. So, start as soon as you bring them home. You need to work on the fundamentals such as housebreaking and basic commands such as "Sit" and "Stay", all of which we will cover in this book. You should also work on stopping your dog's jumping behavior as they may accidentally knock something over in the house as well as teaching them to walk on a loose leash. I admit, it is a lot of work, but you have plenty of time to teach everything. There is no need to tackle everything all at once. Keep your dog's training sessions short and fun. Puppies learn new commands and behavior quickly and you can capitalize on their learning capacity even more by using positive reinforcement training techniques.

Chewing

It is a dog's nature to chew on pretty much everything in its path. If you catch your dog chewing on your favorite pair of sneakers or the table leg, then perhaps you forgot to puppy-proof your own home. Get everyone in the house on board in this project. Leave nothing for the dog to chew on if it can chew on it, no matter how strange it may seem. You could literally save a dog's life just by puppy-proofing your home. This is also why crates are useful as they keep your pup contained, out of trouble. As an alternative, give your dog some good quality chew toys. Just make sure that they are safe. I read a story quite recently about a dog dying from intestine damage because she chewed (and swallowed) on a rope toy that broke. You can also get your puppy some food puzzles and interactive toys to keep them occupied. As your dog is playing with chew toys, it is a good opportunity to teach it the "drop it" command just in case you need to stop them from ingesting inappropriate or harmful items.

Spaying or Neutering

First-time dog owners are not sure when they should spay or neuter their puppy. You should do so before your dog reaches sexual maturity (around five to six months old) so you can prevent unwanted offspring. Some larger breeds can benefit if you spay or neuter them later. Consult your vet about this.

Grooming

Animals can clean themselves, but your puppy can benefit from thorough grooming. If you are wondering when you should do so, the answer is right now. If you introduce your pup to nail trims, brushing, and bathing, it will be much more comfortable with being groomed as it grows up. Do not wait until its an adult because it will be difficult. The key here is to give your pup treats and praise as well as keeping the grooming sessions short.

Size

How big your puppy will grow depends on its breed. Great Danes can weigh more than a hundred pounds as they are one of the giant breeds. These pups can take up to two years to reach their full size. On the flip side, Chihuahuas reach their full size in a year at most and weigh only six pounds. Male dogs are often larger than female ones. In some cases, the size is not so clear-cut because you may get a cross-breed pup than a purebred one. If so, then predicting the size is trickier. As a rule of thumb, the larger their paws are, the larger they will grow. Then again, this is not always accurate so take this advice with a grain of salt.

Eating

The question of how much you should feed your dog is also a tricky one. It depends on the nutrient content and digestibility of the food. Certain dog foods are more nutritious and energy-dense than others, so you should feed your dog less than the usual amount. You should also take the size of your pup into consideration. Small breed puppies such as Chihuahuas might need to eat more frequently to prevent low blood sugar (hypoglycemia) which can be fatal. Not only that, food size and hardness are just as crucial. In our example, Chihuahuas should eat small-kibble food because they have thin teeth. So, feed your small dogs a commercial diet specially created for small dogs. On the other hand, giant-breed puppies require larger but less frequent meals. However, they are also at risk of overfeeding. A lot of people made the mistake of filling the bowl to the brim to help their pups grow big and strong. It's a well-meaning move, but a bowl-full is a lot of calories that can lead to skeletal disorders. If you have a particularly large puppy, feed them dog food that is specifically designed for large puppies. As always, consult your vet to know how much and how often you should feed your dog.

Chapter 3: 5-Step Process to Crate Training

Crate training is a useful tool to have if you've trained your puppy properly. It gives your puppy a sense of stability and safety when you need to put them in a cage. Moreover, it also provides you with a way to establish order and rule in your own home. If you implement crate training properly, it is a win for everyone involved, especially your puppy.

The Crate Philosophy

Your puppy should perceive the crate as its den. Dogs are naturally den animals. In the wild, the den is a safe space for your dog where it can rest, sleep, or fall back to without the fear of danger. For a domesticated pup, the crate serves as a safe haven. Initially, it will see it as confinement which it despises. However, if you introduce and use it correctly, the crate is where your dog willingly chooses to sleep, hide, or simply hang around in because it's their own space.

Why Crate Training is Beneficial

There are many reasons why crate training your dog is a good idea.

House Training

Since you want your dog to treat their crate like how a wild dog would their den. Your puppy will not soil the crate if it sees it as its den. Therefore, you can be assured that your dog will relieve itself outside when you let them out. Of course, there are many other methods of house training your puppy, crate training aligns with your dog's instinct. You just need to take your puppy out of the crate at regular intervals so it can relieve itself elsewhere. That way, your puppy will learn that it needs to take care of its business outside pretty easily.

Transporting

When you familiarize your puppy with the crate early on, house training is only a stone throw away. Not only that, your dog will be comfortable with their future means of transportation. No longer will they bark, whine, or struggle inside the crate. This saves both you and your dog a lot of time and frustration. The crate is the best way to transport your pup, whether it is a short trip to the vet or a long road trip.

Teaching

Dogs, just like humans, need rules to understand their place and boundaries. Crate training is the best way to start introducing your dog to those boundaries and establishing a hierarchy in your home. Your pup will learn early on what it can and cannot do. When you place your pup in a crate when you are away, or when you are otherwise occupied, you restrict its access to the rest of the house so he cannot go ham on your furniture, shows, or soil your rug. When you let your pup have the run of the house, it will always be at a time when you are attentive and can reprimand them appropriately. That way, your pup learns immediately that the crate is its very own space and the rest of the house is yours.

Choosing the Right Crate

As like anything in life, not all crates are the same. There are many crates to choose from and they are all best suited for different situations and dogs. The two best ones are plastic and metal crates.

Plastic Crates

Plastic crates are more for transportation purposes than an in-house den for your pup. They provide less visibility and ventilation. However, they are great if you travel often and take your dog with you because all airlines require your pup to be placed in this crate to be transported. Plastic crates are also useful if your pup needs more security because it is more secluded compared to metal dog crates. You can use plastic crates too if your home has a high level of activity (such as on-the-go kiddos) because they give your pup more privacy.

Metal Crates

These wire, metal crates are a favorite among dog owners for many reasons. These crates have a mesh-like, collapsible structure, making them very convenient because you can just disassemble and transport on a whim. Moreover, they provide a high level of visibility and ventilation for your pup in the crate. Just like plastic creates, metal crates are easy to clean too in case your dog soils them by accident. They may not look like it, but they are sturdy and escape proof, making them an ideal choice for growing dogs. You can just get a large metal dog crate and close off the extra space with dividers, only removing them as your dog grows.

A Note on Crate Size

No matter what crate you choose, you need to make sure that your pup has enough room in there. If it cannot stand up and turn around, then it is too small. On the other hand, do not buy one that is so large that your pup can just soil one corner and sleep in the other. This would make your house training efforts go down the drain.

Personally, I suggest you get a metal crate in your home and a plastic crate for transportation. The metal crate is ideal in your home because you can customize its size with a movable divider. You need to buy new and larger plastic crates as your dog grows anyway.

Training Process

Depending on your dog's age, temperament and past experiences (or traumas), it can take days or even weeks to successfully crate train your dog. You need to keep two things in mind while crate training. First, the crate itself should be perceived (by your dog) to be a place of safety and should elicit pleasant emotions from your dog. Second, the training process should be in a series of small steps. So, do not go too fast.

Step 1: Introduce Your Dog to the Crate

Start by placing the crate in your home where everyone spends a lot of time in, such as the family room. Make the crate appear friendly by placing a soft blanket or towel in there. Take the door off and let the dog explore the crate at its own pace. Certain dogs will be curious and go in and sleep there right away. If yours isn't one of them, do the following:

- Bring your dog to the crate and talk to them in a positive and happy tone of voice. Don't put your dog in the crate; just near it so your dog is aware that the crate is there. Make sure the crate door is open and secured. You don't want the door to fall down and hit your dog as it will frighten them.
- Encourage your pup to enter the crate by dropping treats around the crate. Your dog should approach and eat the treats. Drop more just inside the door and then all the way inside. If your dog is still anxious and refuses to go all the way into the crate, that's fine. There is no need to force your pup to enter it.
- Rinse and repeat the previous step until your dog calmly enters the crate fully to get the food. If treats fail to get their attention, try putting their favorite toy in the crate. Remember, your dog may need several days before it is familiar with the crate.

Step 2: Feed Your Dog Meals in the Crate

After your dog is more familiar with the crate, it is time to convince your pup that the place is its den. Start by feeding them near the crate first to establish a pleasant association with the crate:

- If your dog enters the crate calmly when you start this step, then place the food dish at the back of the crate.
- If your puppy is still reluctant, note how far they are willing to go and place the food dish there. Do not force your pooch to go further inside because they will become fearful or anxious. Every time you feed them, put the dish a little further back and work your way until your dog can eat at the deepest end of the crate.
- When your pup is finally comfortable eating in his crate, you can close the door while they are eating. For the first few days, open the door as soon as your puppy finished eating. From there, try leaving the door closed a few minutes longer. The goal is to make your dog patient enough to stay in the crate for about ten minutes after eating.
- If your dog starts to whine to be let out, then you may increase the length of time too quickly. So, try to leave them for a shorter time period next time. I also want to point out that you should not let your dog out immediately as it is whining. If you do that, your dog will learn that the way to get out of the crate is to whine, so they will keep doing it. So, don't let your dog out unless it stops whining.

Step 3: Practice with Longer Crating Periods

After your dog is comfortable with eating inside their crate, the next step is to confine them in there for a short time while you are home.

- Start by calling your pup over to the crate and give them a treat

- Give them a command to enter the crate. I personally use "kennel" as the command. Also, encourage your pup to enter by pointing to the inside of the crate while holding a treat in your hand.

- When your dog enters the crate, praise and give them a treat. Close the door.

- Sit quietly near the crate for ten minutes or so. Then, get up and go into another room for a few minutes. Repeat one more time before letting your dog out of the crate.

- Repeat the previous step many times and gradually increase the length of time you leave your dog in the crate and the length of time you go elsewhere.

- After several days, your dog should be able to sit quietly inside the crate for about half an hour with you mostly out of sight. Then, you can start leaving them crated when you are away for a short time. This step can take several days or weeks.

Step 4: Crating Your Dog When You Leave

After your dog is accustomed to staying inside the crate for half an hour without being anxious or afraid, you can leave it in there for a short period of time when you leave the house.

- Put it in the crate using the command you used previously and give your pup a treat. I suggest you leave some safe toys in there with them as well so it can entertain itself while you are away.

- Try to vary the moment for your "getting ready to leave" routine that your dog is in the crate. While your pup should not be crated for a long period of time before you leave, you can still put them in there between five to twenty minutes before leaving.

- Do not make your departure longer than it should, let alone emotional. It should be short and simple. Praise your dog and give it a treat for entering the cage. Then leave quietly.

When you finally arrive home again, your dog will be super excited. I understand that it's adorable to see them barking and jumping around because your pup is showing how much it misses you. However, for the sake of your pooch, I advise against rewarding your dog by reflecting their enthusiasm. Doing so will make your dog anxious over when you will arrive home. Instead, keep your arrivals low-key. Moreover, your pup may start to associate crating with being left alone at this stage. To counter this, continue to crate your dog for short periods now and again when you are home.

Step 5: Crate your Dog at Night

Start with the usual command and a treat. At the start, I suggest you put the crate in your bedroom or close by in the hallway. Your puppy needs to go outside to take care of business several times during the night, and you want to be able to hear your puppy whine to let them outside. Other than that, having the crate nearby prevents your dog from seeing it as social isolation.

When your dog is comfortable sleeping in its crate at night close to you, you can start to move the crate gradually to somewhere you prefer. Of course, I would still suggest having your dog as close as possible because even when you two are sleeping, being close to each other strengthens the bond between you and your pet.

Other Tips and Things You Need to Know

Of course, crate training is not as simple as I have pointed out. There are plenty of complications along the way that can confuse even the veteran dog owners.

Whining

This is one potential problem. If your dog whines or cries while it is in the crate at night, it can be tricky to determine whether it is whining to be let out or to do its business. If you have followed the training above and got the results as described, then your dog should not have been rewarded for whining in the past by being released from the crate. This is good because your dog should stop whining after a while if you continue to ignore them. If your dog is just testing you, then they should stop whining soon. Do not yell or pound on the crate as your dog will associate the crate with negative emotions.

If the whining continues after you have ignored your dog for several minutes, then perhaps it really needs to go. If it responds and becomes excited, take it outside so it can do its business. This should be brief because this is not playtime. If you know for sure that your dog is just testing you, just ignore them until the whiling stops. I understand how heart-wrenching it is to hear that pitiful whine. I too had to steel my resolve many times when my new dogs do this to me. However, never give in to their whining. If you do, you will end up teaching your dog to whine loud and long just to get what they want. I had an unpleasant experience with one of my dogs when I was young. The amount of time it took to crate train them again was ridiculous.

If you have gone through the training steps properly without rushing, you should not encounter this problem too often. If this gets out of hand and becomes unbearable and unmanageable, I suggest you start over.

Separation Anxiety

Separation anxiety occurs when your dog becomes too attached to you and becomes very stressed when you leave them alone. It is a lot worse than whining when you leave or a bit of house destruction when you are out. It is so serious that some dog owners become frustrated with their dog and give them up.

It is no use trying to remedy this problem using the crate. While it may prevent your dog from destroying the house while you are gone, it is prone to injuring itself in a desperate attempt to escape. Not only that your dog will be hurt but it may start to associate the crate with isolation, which ruins your crate training progress. Such a problem requires counterconditioning and desensitization procedures. I recommend you consult a professional animal-behavior specialist for help. However, you can still use the crate to help your dog to get comfortable being alone if it has not developed separation anxiety. I recommend you start practicing this as soon as you get your puppy. I will cover this in chapter 11.

What to Avoid

We have previously discussed these, but here they are again for your convenience:

- Do not rush crate training. It is frustrating to go slow, true, but you need to be sure that the crate is a place where your dog is genuinely happy to stay in.
- Do not yell or pound on the crate if your dog is whining. This is counterintuitive because your dog will not be as eager to enter the crate.
- Do not give in when your dog is whining or their behaviors worsen. Your dog can throw a tantrum and you do not want to reinforce such negative behaviors by giving it what it wants.
- Do not use the crate as a form of punishment. Again, you want your dog to associate the crate as a safe haven so your dog is comfortable staying in there.

Chapter 4: Powerful Potty Training

To make it clear from the get-go, potty training and house training are the same. Other than crate training, house training is yet another thing you need to do to help your four-legged canine companion acquaint with its new home. The entire success of house training depends on consistency, patience, and positive reinforcement. You want to instill good habits and build a loving, meaningful bond with your pet.

The training process should take you between four to six months, but certain puppies may need up to a year. The dog's size can help determine how long it will take. For example, smaller breeds have smaller bladders as well as higher metabolisms. This requires them to go outside more frequently to take care of business. That means they will get to do house training more frequently, resulting in quicker success. Your puppy's past experience and living conditions may also be another predictor. You may need to help your pup break old habits before establishing more desirable ones.

Another thing worth mentioning is that setbacks are to be expected. Do not be discouraged by these. So long as you continue to maintain a management program that includes taking your pup out at the first sign that they need to go and offering them a reward, they will learn eventually.

When to Begin?

Experts recommend that you start house training when your pup is between twelve to sixteen weeks old. By then, it can control its bladder and bowel movements well enough to learn how to hold it in.

If your pup is older than twelve weeks when you bring it home and it has been eliminating in its crate (probably even eating its waste), then house training might take longer. If so, you need to reshape the dog's behavior again through encouragement and reward.

Housetraining Steps

If you have crate trained your puppy as I have covered in the previous chapter, then you have already done the first step, which is to confine the pup to a defined space such as a crate, a room, or a leash. Doing so teaches your pup that it needs to go outside to do its business. From there, you can start to introduce more and more space in the house where it can roam around.

Follow these steps when you start to housetrain your puppy:

- Keep its eating schedule precise and regular. Take away its food between meals. Your dog needs to know exactly when they should eat.

- Take your puppy out to eliminate first thing in the morning, then once every 30 minutes to an hour, and last thing before it sleeps. Make sure to take them out after meals or after it wakes up from a nap.
- Whenever you take your dog out, make sure to take them to the same spot all the time. Its scent from the past will prompt them to go at a precise spot.
- Until your pup is housetrained properly, stay with them outside.
- After your pooch eliminates outside, give it praise or a treat. Since you are already outside, a short walk around the neighborhood is not a bad idea for a reward.

Using a Crate to Housetrain a Puppy

A crate can also be used to housetrain your puppy, in the short term anyway. It allows you to keep an eye on them when it shows signs that it needs to go. It also serves to teach your dog to hold it as it does not want to soil its own den. It will learn to wait until you let them outside.

Here are a few guidelines for using a crate:

- Make sure the crate is large enough for your dog. They should be able to stand up, turn around, and lie down in it. It should not be so big that they can use one corner as a bathroom.
- If you use the crate for more than two hours at a time, make sure that your puppy has access to fresh water. So, put a dispenser in there. This is also another reason why you should use a metal crate because you can easily attach a dispenser.
- Using a crate is a bad idea if your puppy eliminates in it. It could mean many things. Your dog may have bad habits from the shelter or pet store where it came from; it may not be let outside enough; the crate could be too big; it could be too young to hold it in.

Tips for Potty Training

Other than what I have described above, there are seven more suggestions you should take into consideration to increase your chance of success.

Keep to a Single Spot

As I have mentioned at the start of this chapter, potty training requires consistency. So, before you even begin potty training your new pal, think of where you want them to go outside of the house. Do you have a yard? Good. Take them to a place where they can get there quickly from the door. If you live in an apartment, you need to identify natural, easy-to-access ground that is not in the way of foot traffic or cars.

After determining where you want your dog to go, make sure to take them there every time it wants to do its business. Dogs can smell its territory so it already knows exactly where if you just show them the way. Rinse and repeat and habit will guide your dog to the same spot without fail. Consistency is important here.

Learn the Signs

Dogs don't speak our language, but they always show visible signs of when they need to eliminate. Thankfully, they are rather overt so you can easily tell if you keep an eye out for them. Take your pup outside immediately to its potty spot if you notice any of the following:

- Smelling its rear
- Walking in circles
- Barking or scratching at the door (the one that leads to its potty spot)
- Sniffing the floor
- Squatting

If you see the final sign, it may be a bit too late. Still, be ready to open the door anyways so your dog knows that it can go to its usual spot now. Chances are that it will make it in time before it goes in the wrong place.

You will need to take your dog outside when you see any of these signs. So, try to plan ahead. I suggest keeping a leash right at the door so you can put it on and get them out as quickly as possible. After learning where its potty area is, your dog will go to that same spot on its own. Just make sure it is the same spot every time your dog needs to relieve itself.

Keep Meal Time Consistent

When you are housetraining a puppy, make sure to keep all meal and snack times properly scheduled. This is useful for two main reasons. First, scheduled meals will teach your dog when it can expect to eat throughout the day. Second, if you are feeding your dog at specific times, you can bring it to its potty area expecting it to go soon after mealtimes.

Water Bowl

If your dog drinks a lot of water, it may need to go out more frequently. To prevent accidents, make sure to take your pup outside shortly after it drinks water during the potty training phase. That way, your dog can be in the right place at the right time.

Go Outside Often

If you want to ensure that your dog takes care of business outside, you need to take them outside regularly as well. As previously mentioned, take your dog outside:

- First thing in the morning;
- Last thing before bed;
- Once every thirty minutes to one hour throughout the day (especially for young puppies)
- After feeding and drinking (within thirty minutes).

You can lengthen the time between trips outside when you are confident that your dog will hold it in and tell you when it needs to go outside. Getting your dog to take care of business before bedtime is a good idea as well. Your 3 a.m. self will be grateful for it. I personally dread having to wake up at odd hours just to let the dog outside.

Praise Often

Everyone likes to be told that they are doing a good job. This is a positive reinforcement approach that will help your puppy in the housetraining process. I recommend you start with giving your dog treats for every success "business" taken care of and gradually moving to saying a simple "good job" followed up with some pats. Whatever you do, just make sure your dog knows that you appreciate its efforts to do the right thing.

Address Accidents Calmly

Accidents may happen, especially during the early stage of the housetraining process. Whenever your dog eliminates in your home, be calm when you address the situation. Simply redirect your dog outside to its potty spot immediately. Remember that accidents tend to happen during the training process anyway. Be patient and never give up. Do not punish your dog for accidents because it can worsen the situation and may result in more accidents at home. Some dog owners told me that they got so annoyed at their dogs that they shoved their dogs' noses into the excrement. Let me tell you, it never ends well for both the owners and the dog as it only makes things worse.

If you happen to catch your puppy in the act, clap loudly to tell them that it has done something wrong. Then, take them outside gently by the collar or calling it. After it is done, praise them or give them a small treat. While you are outside, it is worth staying there with your dog longer. It may take the time to explore the area so it can go there on his own next time.

After an accident, make sure you clean up the area as quickly and as best as possible. It is crucial that the place remains spotless to eliminate any scents so no further accidents can take place in the same place. If your dog smells urine or feces in your home, it will think that it is fine to relieve itself inside in the future. You don't want that to happen. So long as your dog knows where to take care of business, it will have fewer problems. When you clean the soiled spot, make sure you use pet-safe cleaners and keep your dog away from the area while it dries. I recommend you clean up using enzymatic cleanser rather than an ammonia-based cleaner to minimize odors that might attract your puppy to commit the same mistake.

Accidents are common in puppies up to a year old. There are many reasons for the accident. Perhaps the housetraining is not complete. Maybe the puppy is still unfamiliar with its environment. Just keep on training your pup. However, if the training seems to have no effect, I suggest you visit the vet just in case it has a medical issue that needs to be addressed. Frequent urinating or defecating in the house can be a symptom of a larger issue. In most cases, they might suggest a simple change to your training routine or a change to their food. However, if it is something serious, you will be glad that you called sooner rather than later.

Preparing for Various Situations

There are many situations that you should be prepared for during the potty training process. Below are some of the scenarios you need to be ready for:

Introduce Your Puppy to New People and Places

I personally committed the same mistake when I was an inexperienced dog owner. I got a new pup and I wanted to show it off to my friends and family. Unfortunately for my poor pup, the excitement was too much for its bladder to handle. I tell you this so you don't have to be caught off-guard. So, prepare for this situation by making sure you let them take care of business before you introduce them to anyone new during their training phase. This includes meeting new people and seeing new places.

Moreover, if you take your pup to your friend's or family's house with other dogs, it may sniff around and try to mark its own territory. Dogs urinate to mark their territory, so you don't want that to happen in someone else's house. So, keep an eye on them and take them outside frequently. It can mark as many bushes it wants outside the house.

Traveling with a House Training Puppy

Raising a puppy is a big responsibility, but that does not mean that your life needs to revolve around them. You might be tempted to take a road trip to an exciting place, and that is completely fine. If you do decide to go somewhere far, you need to decide whether or not you are going to take your pup with you or have someone watch them while you are away.

If you want to take your pooch with you, then you need to take them outside before you leave and stop once every couple hours to let your dog do its business. You and your passengers do not want to put up with the odor of dog urine or worse, during the whole trip.

If you decide to have someone watch your dog, make sure to let them know that it is in the middle of potty training. Give them step-by-step and clear instructions on how you have been working with them so far so the other person can keep the training consistent. Confusing your dog with inconsistent training regimen can ruin your entire progress.

Planning for Bad Weather

You will need to deal with bad weather during your dog's potty training phase eventually, so be prepared for it. If it is raining, you cannot expect your dog to hold it in until the sky clears. So, have a large umbrella handy. I suggest putting it close to the door next to the leash. I suggest you have a towel to wipe off their feet after they have taken care of business. You do not want to have mud all over your floor. If it is snowing outside, your new pup may be curious about this new white thing all over the ground. It is fine if curiosity gets the best of your dog. it can explore and play in it a little. Still, it can get cold just like us, so you should usher them to their usual spot as soon as possible. If it is covered in snow, you should grab a shovel and clear out a path for them so it can relieve itself in a more familiar surrounding. We want to be consistent when training your pup.

Moving

If you plan to move within a year or two, I don't recommend you get a dog now because it will be too tedious to retrain your dog in the new home. However, if you find yourself with a new puppy or a well-trained adult dog and you need to move, keep in mind that your dog will want to explore its new surroundings and the act of moving itself will be stressful for them. In its new home, it may try to mark its new territory. So, to help them acclimate to their new surrounding, immediately take them to the spot where you want themto do business just like how you would back at your previous location. Take your dog frequently to this spot and give it rewards and praises if it relieves itself there. This is to rebuild its good association with good behaviors. If your dog has been housetrained successfully before you move, then it should be quick for your dog to get used to its new bathroom. Just make sure you follow the same housetraining routine.

After moving, I recommend you restrict your dog to a certain portion of your house first before gradually introducing it to new areas after it becomes more familiar with its new bathroom routine. You do not want to find a nasty surprise at the other end of your house to which you did not know it had access.

Whatever you do, make sure that your furry friend remains calm during the entire ordeal. An excited, scared, or stressed pup may cause accidents in the home, no matter how well-trained it is.

Chapter 5: 5 Essential Commands

In this chapter, we will look at some of the essential skills your puppy needs to pick up. Some of which include crate training, potty training, and basic commands (Sit, lay down, come, stay, and no). These are the foundation and it helps condition your puppy, as in readying it for more complicated commands.

There are a few things you need to know before you start teaching your puppy:

- Be patient
- Be consistent, both for commands (consistent voice and gesture, more on that in chapter 8) and rewards
- Do not push your dog too hard at the start
- Find somewhere quiet to train your pup, far away from distractions
- Make the learning sessions short and simple
- Make your training consistent and regular
- Do not punish your dog, in any circumstances
- Start by practicing at home or the backyard first before exercising commands publicly
- Reward your pup after each successful trick or command
- Show your pup what you want them to know – do not use force
- Time is of the essence – teach your dog a new command as soon as it learns the previous one properly
- Spice things up – make the training fun and entertaining
- Get involved in the training exercise with the dog – it needs someone to play with as well

With that out of the way, let's go over the five essential dog commands that every dog owner needs:

The 5 Commands

Remember that your dog needs to learn basic discipline and respect which are defined by the energy and direction that you give to your dog. Discipline helps your dog learn new tricks and commands quickly as it can avoid dog behavioral problems.

Other than that, remember that any of the commands I mention here, if applied appropriately, can be entertaining for both you and your dog. That way, the learning process is much more enjoyable. Without further ado, let us go over these essential commands:

"Sit" Command

To teach this command, put the dog treat close to your dog's nose so it can smell it better, then move the treat up. Your pup should follow the treat, but make sure you move it high enough so it cannot catch the treat.

Your dog will sit down so it can pull its head high to follow the treat. When this happens, give the command "Sit" and give them the treat and some pats. Rinse and repeat until the dog learns to properly execute this command.

This is a necessary command because you can use it to prevent your dog from doing anything annoying such as getting into trouble with other dogs in the street, or jumping on people when you are taking it for walks. With this command, your dog will sit and not move from its position. You can teach another command such as "Okay" or "Brake" to tell the dog that it can get up now.

"Stay" Command

This command is a step-up from "Sit". So, have your dog sit and put the treat close to the nose, then give the "Stay" command. Then, move awaya few steps from your dog. If the dog stays in the same spot, offer them a treat. If not, say "No" and move away from them again. That way, it knows if it is doing something wrong and whether it did something right.

Repeat this exercise several times daily, particularly if you own a hyper-energetic dog. This command challenges your pup to practice self-control, which is crucial.

"Down" Command

This can be a tricky command because it challenges the dog to put itself in a passive or submissive position. It challenges your dog's pack hierarchy.

To teach this command, get some delicious treats that smell good and hold it in a closed hand. Move your hand close to the dog's nose. As your dog smells it, move your hand to the floor. Your dog should have its nose glued to your hand. Then, move your hand along the floor, away from your dog slowly so your dog follows your hand until it lays down on its stomach. When that happens, give the command "Down" and give them the treat.

Repeat this exercise every day. If your dog tries to grab the treat forcefully, retract your hand quickly and say "No". Try again until it executes the command successfully before giving it the treat. Tell the dog to get up with "Okay" or "Brake".

"Come" Command

To teach this command, start by putting a collar and a leash on your dog then take a few steps back from them. Then, ask it to "come" towards you and pull on the leash gently. The moment it approaches you, give it a treat so it knows that this is an exercise.

You need to repeat this exercise many times daily. Release your dog with an "Okay" or "Yes" and show it your affection.

This command helps protect your dog by preventing it from getting into trouble with other dogs. If it runs away in the streets or chases something or someone, you can get them back using this command.

"No" Command

To teach this command, start by placing a treat on the ground and keeping the dog leashed as you walk slowly towards the treat. The moment your dog becomes interested in the treat and tries to grab it, give the "no" command and pull the dog back slightly. When it approaches and watches you, offer them a treat and say "Yes", and give them some pats. Rinse and repeat daily and your dog should understand the command eventually.

This command is very useful because you can use it to keep your dog away from improper behavior or dangerous objects at home, street, or anywhere else to protect them from harm.

Chapter 6: 6 Weeks to Master the Fundamentals

Puppies and dogs do not come into our home knowing the house rules. If you introduce a new puppy into your home, taking the time to properly train them will be beneficial to both you and your dog. I have compiled a quick 6-to-8 week schedule so you can get your dog to master the fundamentals.

First Month

This is the most crucial month of puppy training. Schedule a wellness exam with the vet as soon as possible to get the first or second vaccination in. In some cases, the animal shelter or breeder may have already vaccinated the pup prior to giving them to you. If you live in the United States, it is now illegal to sell or give away puppies younger than eight weeks old. So, read up before you get one below that age. I recommend you get one around eight weeks old though because the pup has enough time to learn basic social etiquette and skills with its mother and siblings. More on that in bite inhibition in chapter 10. Make sure your pup is excited to go to the vet by rewarding them with quality meat or delicious treats at every vet visit.

After getting the first round of vaccinations, it is time to start puppy training right off the bat. You can start introducing them to the world around them by taking them to safe places for socialization such as the neighbor's house with young children, a dog training center, or local shops that allow dogs inside. If your pup is not vaccinated, do not take it to areas with a lot of dog traffic such as parks or dog retail stores as it can contract some deadly preventable diseases.

According to research, there is a limited window of time to familiarize a dog to new events, people, and things. For puppies, we have about 12 weeks after it was born to give it positive exposure to our world. Other studies suggest that 16 weeks is the cut-off time.

Introductions are Crucial

By the time your pup comes into your home, you've already missed eight weeks, so we are starting out a bit late here unless you got your pup from a great breeder or shelter that have given them training and socialization prior to adoption.

The first month is all about introduction. Slowly and positively introduce them to as many new things as you can find, especially small children, cats, men with beards, different surfaces, people walking that are dressed in different attires, and other friendly puppies (in this case, make sure you have at least one round of vaccination in), and older dogs, car rides, and other things that do not intimidate your dog.

Try to introduce your dog to at least five new stimuli a day, throughout the day. It won't understand new, potentially harmful or scary things with just a brief introduction. So you need repetition to get it to familiarize with whatever it is you are introducing to it. You can also make your dog's learning experience fun by using something fun or delicious for them.

As long as you do not force your pup into new situations, people, or objects, you should be good to go. Give them time to sniff and get to know other pups or people to help them build confidence and resilience. Force is never a good option in any animal training, and it is going to cause more harm to your pup.

Importance of Touch

There is one thing human babies and puppies' development have in common: touch. They both need to understand that touch is not aversive or a threat. If you miss this crucial lesson in puppy training, you may not be able to convince them ever again that touch is comfort and a sign of affection, not danger. When that happens, we call it dogs feral. So, make sure your pup is comfortable with touch.

House Training

For housetraining, the first phase is going to be tiring for you. You will need to take your pup outside every few hours, including overnight. So, it is best to set an alarm. Try your best to avoid situations in which your pup needs to go to the bathroom, and the only option is to soil inside the house. Moreover, reward your pup generously whenever your pup goes outside. Personally, I keep young puppies with me 24/7 for the first three days and they are housetrained within 72 hours.

Second Month

When your pup has its vaccinations, take some time to enroll in a force-free, positive puppy behavior reinforcement class with an experienced dog trainer who has a hygienic training facility. This is a socialization class that your puppy needs to learn bite inhibition, among other things.

There are so many things to do in the first month that you will most likely only have time to find a puppy class in the second month. Make sure your pup gets in a class before it hits the 12-week mark. Of course, that does not mean that your dog cannot learn anything new after 12 weeks. It's just that they learn a lot faster in that 2-month period, especially for young pups.

Socialization and obedience are crucial for a well behaved dog, but they need to have a human companion who can help ease them into our world. That human is you, of course. Try your very best to squeeze in socialization because this is going to be very important later on. Other than that, you can also teach them some crucial commands that I covered in the previous chapter.

When you get your dog to socialize, keep them away from rude dogs. Make sure it gets to mingle with other, well-behaved dogs and puppies before that 2-month period.

Bottom Line

Puppies, just like babies, require a lot of time and effort if you want them to grow up well behaved. Though tedious, the reward is so worth it. You can take your dog anywhere with you without worrying about them misbehaving and you will be glad that you put in the time now to properly train them.

Dos and Don'ts of Positive Reinforcement

Positive reinforcement is a very effective tool to train your dog, but it is not as straightforward as praising your dog for everything that it gets right. If you want to make the most out of positive reinforcement training, you need to follow the dos and don'ts:

Do...

Immediately Praise and Reward Desired Behavior

Animals, especially dogs, live in the moment. They are not capable of thinking ahead, so your response should also be immediate if you want your training to be effective. This applies to both giving treats and affection. You should reward whenever your pup does something that you want them to do. If you are potty training a dog, reward them every time it does its business outside. Make sure you reward your pup every time it gets a command right.

Keep the Training Short and Fun

The idea is to get your dog to understand that good things come its way when it obeys you. As we said earlier though, dogs cannot tolerate boring training for long. So, try to make your training sessions short and fun. If possible, try to end the training on a good note by finishing it up with a successful command and a treat.

Wean from Treats

Speaking of treats, while they are necessary to entice your dog to listen to you, there is a risk of overfeeding if you rely on them too much. It is okay to use them in the starting phase of the training, but you should wean your dog off of them because they may not obey your command unless you have a treat ready. Instead, replace treats with affections and pats. Eventually, your pup should do what you want just to make you happy. In a way, your smile is its reward. You can also associate a reward with certain sounds such as "Good boy/girl!" or a click from the clicker (more on that in Chapter 11), accompanied by a treat. Eventually, you can take away the treat and your dog should still respond to the sound.

Don't...

Make Things Complicated

If you want your dog to fetch its toy, don't use the command "Fetch Mr. Goofy". It is long and overcomplicated. Instead, just say "Fetch" and point to one of the toys. When it does fetch you the toy, reward them. If your commands or training routine are too complicated, your dog will never be able to learn anything. Keep it short and simple.

Show inconsistency

Along that line, make sure you are consistent if you want your puppy to have a specific behavior. For instance, if you reward your dog for not jumping on the couch, you cannot let them come up there and give them pats. Doing so will only confuse your dog about what you really want. Moreover, and this is a common mistake, everyone else in the house also needs to follow the same rules. Your poor pup will be so confused if it has to remember what it needs to do for everyone. This also applies to command. If you say "Sit" to get your dog to sit, others cannot use the command "Sit down" and expect your dog to sit.

Stop Correcting Your Dog

Another big mistake that I see dog owners make that often come with positive reinforcement is that they cannot say no to their dogs. I understand that they are adorable, and I made the same mistake in the past, but you need to correct wrongful behavior. Just make sure you keep the correction time separate from positive reinforcement time. Just like children, we need to teach our dogs discipline.

Chapter 7: Training Your Puppy Daily

In this chapter, I will show you how you can incorporate certain daily routines with command training to hasten your dog learning process.

Sit and Stay

There are three occasions in which you can use these commands daily to reinforce your dog's learning:

Pre-Meal

This is a great time to get your dog to practice sitting as well as "Stay". These are the foundation for basic obedience but a solid "Stay" will keep your dog still, preventing them from digestive problems or poisonings when you accidentally drop harmful foods or medications, or when you encounter them on walks. So, whenever you feed your dog, do the following:

- Before placing down the food bowl, ask your dog to sit.
- Once it does that, give them praise (and a treat if your dog is just starting practicing this command), but do not let your dog eat its meal yet.
- Then, ask it to stay.
- If it can remain calm for a few seconds, give them praise and a treat, then let them have their meal.
- You can reinforce this behavior further by feeding, you can feed your dog through an interactive feeder such as Wobbler by Kong, or Dog Tornado by Nina Ottoson. This allows you to extend their training and give them some mental exercise during their meals, so you can get even more mileage out of the training program.

At the Door

Seeing your dog jumping and clinging to you whenever you open the door is cute the first few times, but it can get old quickly. I already mentioned why you should not greet your dog with the same level of energy. So, here are some tips to prevent that from happening:

- Have an air-tight jar of treats outside your front door. Hang it somewhere high enough so that your dog or others cannot reach it.
- Before you walk through the door, grab a few treats.
- When your dog greets you in an excited manner, ask them to sit immediately. Do not give them any more attention until it does what you told them.
- Give your dog praise and some treats as soon as it sits down.

- To capitalize on this exercise, tell other family members and visitors to do the same. With constant and consistent practice, you will have a safer and more pleasant arrival.

Crossing the Street

Growing up, we are taught to look both ways before crossing a street. Why don't we teach our dogs the same thing? What is more important here is the actual stopping and sitting before crossing the intersection, rather than the looking. You get the idea.

- When you are taking your dog out for a walk, ask your dog to sit at each intersection before you cross.
- Give them praise and a treat when they follow your command. Eventually, your dog will learn to be patient and sit at each intersection rather than trying to pull you into the oncoming traffic.
- Just for safety reasons, make sure you and your dog remain a few feet back from the curb rather than right next to the street. Some people may have clever ideas and cut their turn too tight, pulling a tire up over the curb.

7 Tips to Make Training Fun

Training is one of the most important things you can do the moment you get your new puppy. When your dog can behave properly, you have more options for what things you can do with your dog. This opens up new possibilities for you to build your relationship and enrich your's and your dog's life. Learning should not be confined to a certain space, as I'm sure you know by now. So, why not do the same for your dog? You can further reinforce your dog's behaviors throughout the day with additional training.

- Take your dog out on shopping trips. Most stores allow dogs inside, but it is best if you call ahead just to make sure. Once you two are in, you can practice leash manners by asking your dog to sit or stay at one location while you go about your daily business.
- Take your dog out on trips, even short ones. The simple act of getting in and out of the car provides ample opportunities for socialization.
- Practice sitting quietly. You don't want your dog to bark, lunge, jump, let alone bite, other people who walk by. These things can happen right at your doorstep if you are not careful. So, try practicing polite manners for your dog by putting it on a leash, ask them to sit whenever someone shows up at the door. Be prepared to restrain your dog whenever you open the door.
- Practice sit, stay, and down. Your dog loves you and wants to be with you, but there are times when you need to relax undisturbed or want to get things done without distractions. So, use this opportunity to teach your dog to relax and be quiet whenever you go about doing chores or watching TV.

- Practice stay. When you are more confident in your dog, take them to places with a lot of distractions, such as the park or when you pick up your kids from school. Order your dog to sit politely while you watch people walking by.
- Call for them. When you want your dog to eat its lunch, go outside, or come back in when it's barking at a squirrel in your backyard, call its name. This makes them remember their name clearly and train them to turn their attention back to you in case you cannot find them in a busier environment.
- Reward for behaviors. Reward your dog for everything they got right and use every opportunity to practice with your dog. If it likes going out for walks, then make it sit and wait for its leash to be put on. If it wants to play or a treat, ask them to sit or lie down before you give them what it wants.

Chapter 8: Verbal and Visual Cues

You may have problems getting your dog to understand cues. I have that problem too. I asked one of my dogs to sit several times but she never responds. It seems that she did not hear me or was just being stubborn. If that sounds like your dog, then you are not alone in this. Many dog owners have this problem from time to time.

I used to have to repeat the "Sit" command three times so my dog would sit. "Sit! Sit! Sit!" is a command many people use to get their dog to sit down. I personally used it before too, until I found out the hard way that we are actually teaching our dog a delayed sit. When your dog is trained to sit the first time, it will normally sit when you say "Sit" once. However, when you repeat it three times, your dog thinks that the verbal cue has changed to "Sit, sit, sit". So, it will not sit down until you repeat the command three times. This isn't so much of an issue until you need your dog to respond immediately.

Getting Your Dog to Understand You

Because your dog does not speak English, vocal and physical cues are the only means of communication between you two. Even so, your dog can misinterpret a simple gesture. Many things can get lost in translation. So, you need to speak the dog language so your dog can understand you and you can take your time understanding your dog as well.

It all starts by establishing a bond by playing with your dog. Just have fun with them and make sure that both you and your dog spend time making good memories. You can use vocal and physical language to bridge the gap between human and animal.

Some dogs have a harder time understanding humans than others. If yours cannot respond to cues properly, try to change how much you teach them. Many dogs can follow along with human gestures, but yours may not understand what your pointed finger means. But if you say their name, look at them, and then look at where you are pointing, they may be able to follow along and understand what you are trying to tell them.

There are many reasons why your dog has difficulty picking up on cues. Many dog owners often jump the gun and say that their dog's lack of compliance means that it is being disobedient or stubborn. That is not the case at all. In reality, your dog may be too distracted to understand your command, may not feel comfortable doing what you asked them to do in that particular situation, and do not know how to respond.

The last part is often true if you have your dog practice commands at home, and not anywhere else. Just because they will sit down at home when you say so does not mean that they can do the same elsewhere. Just like us, dogs feel different when put in a different environment. We may feel that we need to speak formally and smile in the office, but we throw caution to the wind, jokingly insulting your best friend on the phone while in your pajamas on a lazy Saturday afternoon. The same applies to your dog. You need to teach your dog the same cue in as many different situations and environments as you can. Again, you need to be consistent with your training. That way, the cue, and response become fluent no matter where they are.

How Your Body Language and Attitude Affects Your Dog

If your dog can respond well to vocal cues, then great! However, your body language is just as important when you try to teach your dog new tricks. Active hand gesticulations and body signals pair up well with behaviors that compel your dog to act. Passive behaviors such as turning your back and ignoring your dog's unwanted behavior can be used to tell your dog that you do not approve of what it is doing and that it needs to stop. In some cases, these passive behaviors are more effective than shouting and yelling when it does something you don't approve. The exception, of course, is when your dog is trying to tell you something important.

Your personality also affects your dog's behavior drastically. Since dogs learn to read human nonverbal cues, they are very sensitive to our attentional and emotional states. If you are an extrovert, your dog will match your energy and be more attentive. Unfortunately for my introverted friends, your dog may struggle to understand you because of the inhibited communicative abilities.

Studies have shown that people who suffer from a lack of confidence and being dependent on others often have dogs who have behavior problems. Shy, anxious, tense, or aggressive individuals may incite nervousness, anxiety, and aggression in their dogs. Neurotic or lay owners have dogs who are not as active or responsible. Conscientious handlers have dogs that are easier to teach. The less frequent correction you give to your dog, the more responsive it will be.

Be Clear with Your Cues

So, when you teach your dog new commands, be clear with your gestures and vocal cues. Dogs cannot understand humans, but they can certainly understand the tone and pitch of your voice to understanding what you are feeling. However, when you want your dog to respond to a vocal cue, use a short and simple cue word and pair it with a clear gesture so they can understand what you want them to do.

Certain gestures can be interpreted differently by your dog, especially if it is a stranger doing it or if the dog has a traumatic experience in the past. For instance, hugging, bending over to pet the dog, maintaining eye contact, or kissing can be threatening to your dog if it does not enjoy social contact.

So, if your dog is uncomfortable with the activities I described above, try to get them to familiarize with you. Allow them to come into your space, letting them smell your hand, and only pet it when itwants you to. Doing so makes them feel a lot more comfortable towards you and others.

Hand Gestures

All of us want our dogs to respond to verbal cues such as "Sit" and hand signals reliably. As humans, we primarily use our voices to communicate, although a majority of what we are really trying to say is hidden in our body language. Your dog may see that humans are crazy making weird noises at each other all the time. I certainly understand that because Rex gave me that confused look whenever I talked to him, although heunderstood from my tone and responded appropriately. If I was feeling down, he would nudge my hand to pat him or just sit and reflect my look, timidly sighing as I rambled on and on.

Unlike humans, dogs speak mainly through body language. Other than the difference in barking tone, growls, and whine, you hardly hear your dog making any other noises. But you can tell what your dog is trying to say just by looking at its face and stance. Because dogs understand body language better, they pick up on our gestures much quicker when we teach them sit, down, and other commands.

That does not mean that dogs are deaf to verbal cues. They can easily learn both verbal cues and hand signals. One study shows that dogs can learn more than 160 words through training and observation, so a few commands are not that hard for them. The problem is that we get stuck and our pooch does not seem to fully understand what it is we want them to do. What then, is the problem?

If you have problems with your dog not following commands, then you are not alone. Many dogs I have worked with suffered from what is known as overshadowing. It is when a certain stimulus is unnoticed by your dog because there is a more evident stimulus around. For example, you may tell your dog to sit while lifting their hand. You know what sit means and assume that your dog understands that too until you say it and your dog does not respond. What happened here? Well, your dog understands the sit command. The problem is that your dog only picks up one of those cues. Because dogs understand body language more than verbal cues, they look to your hand first and then your voice. So, your voice is overshadowed by your hand signal.

This is why it is absolutely crucial that you watch what you say and how you gesture as you train your pup. So, how do you approach this problem? You may be wondering how you can teach your dog both verbal and hand signal. Well, you just have to separate the two. It's that simple!

First, you need to remember how you trained your pup. If you used a toy or treat to teach your dog to sit, then get rid of it as soon as possible. To teach your dog to sit using your hand signal, simply move your hand to imitate how you would order your dog to sit with a toy or treat. This time, of course, with an empty hand. If your dog responds four out of five times or more, then your dog already understands the hand signal. Then, you can add a verbal cue.

To achieve this, start by saying your verbal cue first while keeping your body still. Follow up immediately with your hand signal without saying anything else. When your dog sits, give it a reward. Keep doing this until itbecomes proficient. From that point on, the verbal cue serves as a predictor for your dog. In this case, if you say "sit", then your dog knows that you will offer the hand signal to "confirm" your command. It will respond by sitting. Simple!

If your dog becomes proficient enough at sitting when you move your hand back and forth, and you have practiced the command successfully several times, then your dog should be able to anticipate what comes next. When you say "sit", it will assume that it will be followed by your hand gesture and sit even before you give the hand cue. Voila, you have successfully taught your dog the sit command! Now, do that for all the other commands.

Here is a TL; DR version:

- Say the command, then give your hand cue. Wait for your dog to execute the command before rewarding them.
- Repeat in succession up to five times, for five days.
- On the sixth day, say the command, but do not give the hand cue. If your dog executes the command, reward them.
- If it does not execute the command after you repeat the verbal and hand cue combo five more times, then switch to using the verbal cue on the sixth attempt.

You may be surprised to see how easy it is to train your dog using this technique. The key takeaway here is that no matter what you want your dog to learn, it all boils down to how you teach them to get the behavior you want. Using the power of positive reinforcement, your dog can reliably execute the command.

Remember, dogs cannot understand English. If you yell "Down! Down! Down!" before they know what we want them to do, they will associate that command with whatever they are doing. Once your dog learns a behavior, it is hard to unlearn it.

Chapter 9: Spice Up Your Training

In this chapter, I will show you how to make training really fun by using one of the many games and activities that both you and your dog can enjoy. Playing games with your pooch has great physical and mental benefits. They can be active and engaged which will promote their growth into an active dog. It is also a great way for you to strengthen your bond with your pet to create a meaningful relationship. However, it is important to ensure that you do not exacerbate other behavioral issues. I recommend you stick to the games below and have fun.

Tug of War

This is a great game as you can teach your dog to listen to you when it is distracted and excited. It strengthens bonds through play and serves as a great workout for both you and your dog. You may hear people claim that this game incites aggressiveness within dogs as they need to be protective to play this game. That is not the case. Most dogs do not become aggressive when playing this game. In fact, it builds up trust and cooperative skills if you follow certain rules:

- You do not have to win the game. It is best to let your dog win sometimes. Give and take is the best in this relationship.

- Teach your dog the "drop it" or "take it" command before you play this game so they can understand what you mean when you ask them to drop the toy.

- If your dog wins and takes the toy away from you, try to feign disinterest and go do something else. It is a bad idea to chase your dog to try and get the toy from them as it is tiring and can cause aggression. Instead, ignore them until it comes up to you with the toy. Alternatively, grab another toy and put all your attention onto the toy you have. Doing so will make your dog curious and they will drop what it has in its mouth to come and investigate a better toy.

- In certain cases, your dogmay even come directly to you and drop the toy at your feet. When that happens, praise them and continue the game.

- The game should stop on your cue and if it gets too rowdy, ask your dog to drop the toy or drop it yourself. Walk away. Rowdy play can lead to accidents quickly so stop the game.

Hide and Seek

This is a very simple game. If your dog knows how to stay, the game will be much easier. If it doesn't, get a human helper to keep it still while you hide. Then you can call them to come to you or call their name and they should start looking around the house. When it finds you, reward it with a treat or its favorite toy. At the start, I suggest you remain in plain sight in the next room. Later on, when your dog becomes more proficient, start hiding in places that are hard for them to find. What about that other person who helped hold the dog for you? That person can participate too! They can go hide somewhere as the dog is finding you. When it found you, the other person can call to them so it starts the game all over again. This back and forth will hone your dog's ability to seek you out. This is a simple game, but you can only repeat it a few times because your pup will lose interest eventually.

Find the Treats

Speaking of treats, this game is a great way to hone your dog's sense of smell. Consider this a hide-and-seek variant. Except, instead of finding you, your dog has to find the treat. You can use bits of kibble or your dog's favorite treats for this game. If your pup hasn't played this game before, start by placing a treat in plain sight to get your dog used to the idea of the game. It will take a while for your pooch to stop relying solely on visual cues. After a few rounds, you can start putting the treat in secluded areas like behind the couch. Your dog will learn to sniff out those treats eventually.

The Which Hand Game

You can hone your dog's smelling skills by playing this game first then the above to skip past the initial step of breaking your dog's habit of relying on visual. This game is quite common on the internet and you should see many videos of this game already. The premise is very simple. You hide a dog treat in one of your hands and hold them out to your dog in a fist. Let your pup pick which hand the treat is in. If your dog doesn't play nice and tries to mouth at your hands or claw at them, say no, retract your hand, and try again.

The 3-Cup Game

This is yet another nose-training starter game. As you can tell from the name, the premise is just like the previous game. The only difference is that you use three cups, not two hands. Place those cups in a row in front of your dog. Then, take out a treat and put it close to your dog's nose so they can sniff it. This allows them to memorize the scent and focus their eyes on the treat. Place the treat under one of the three cups as your dog is watching. Then gesture to the cups to let your dog have the pick. When itchooses the right cup, give them praise and let them have their treat. After it gets the hang of this game, you can make it more challenging by mixing the cup around after you place the treat.

Go Find or Retrieve

If your dog likes carrying things in its mouth, then this game will be one of their favorite. Even if it doesn't, you can still try to teach your dog to bring your toys to you even though it doesn't like fetching something you throw. This game has an added benefit of teaching your dog how to fetch toys for you to help you tidy up the place.

- Start by placing the toy a few feet away from where your dog is sitting so it can see it. Then, ask it to find it. You can say something like "Go find" and point to the toy. Alternatively, if your dog recognizes each toy by name, you can say the name of the toy or object that you hide and want them to bring to you.
- When it goes to the toy, give it praise even if it doesn't touch it yet. For some dogs, they will not only approach, but also take the toy into their mouth. In any case, repeat the game a few times to reinforce the behavior. If your dog doesn't take the toy into its mouth, continue to give it praise whenever itapproaches the toy and encourage it to pick up the toy.
- Whenever your dog picks up the toy, give them praise and let them play with it for a while. Eventually, they will recognize the "Go find" cue and automatically goes to the toy and pick it up.
- The next step is to encourage your dog to bring it back to you. Give your dog praise when it runs back to you with the toy in its mouth, then again when it brings it to your hand. Take the toy away and give them a treat.
- As your dog becomes more proficient at the game, you can kick things up a notch and hide the toy in different places and send them off on the hunt.

Puppy Ping Pong

Most of the dog owners I have worked with prioritized two behaviors. Learning to come when being called, and learning how to walk on a leash. These form the core of dog behavior. In addition to what dog trainers help you achieve, you can further these behaviors in your dog at home by playing puppy ping pong. This game helps build your dog's reaction to hearing their name and running towards their owner.

This game can have two or more people. The idea is to teach your dog to recognize their name and respond appropriately. Each person will have a handful of delicious treats. Everyone gathers around your dog, standing a short distance away. Then, one at a time, take turns calling the puppy. Be very excited and happy whenever you call the puppy to encourage her to run fast toward you. When the puppy reaches the person calling, touch the dog's collar and give them a reward. Make sure to use the treat sparingly, though. You don't want yourpup picking up too much weight. That is why this exercise can only be done a few times each day. Make sure you touch the collar first before you give them the treat. If you can touch the collar, you can restrain them, which is going to be crucial if you want to get a hold of your dog alongside a busy road. Calling them back to you won't do you any good if it runs off before you can catch them, right?

Have your dog run around a few more times by having another person here and make sure that everyone rewards it the same way. I recommend that you switch to using pats as a form of reward as soon as possible though. You don't want your dog relying on treats to perform a certain command.

Catch Me If You Can

All dog owners can testify to the unending annoyance when their dog picks something up when they shouldn't and immediately makes the run for it when their owner notices. This also applies to when you call your dog, but it does not come to you. Most of us would go to our dog, which prompts them to run. To your dog, this is a fun game of chase. To us, this is an annoyance, especially if this is a serious case. What can we do about this? This is where the game comes in. It turns the table on your puppy and teaches her that it is more fun for them if she were to catch up to you instead of you pursuing them.

Play this game in a safe place such as your home and put them on a leash. Then, move away from them and encourage them to follow you. As it moves towards you, stop moving and let it catch up to you. Give it praise and a reward with a treat. As your dog is enjoying the treat, move away from them again and call them to come to you. Rinse and repeat. The stopping and letting the dog catching up is to prevent your pup from biting at your pant legs or jump at you as you are running.

Chapter 10: Dealing with Negative Behavior

In this chapter, I will go over how you can deal with common negative behaviors that often ended up with puppies being given up. Many of us want our dogs to behave properly but when they don't, we become upset at them. To fix negative behaviors in your four-legged canine friend, we need to understand the reason behind such behaviors. These negative behaviors include excess barking, biting and nipping, chewing things around the house, excessive digging and jumping on people, and dealing with dog's separation anxiety.

Preventing Barking

We all used to go through this problem. Maybe your dog is barking at a passing squirrel… at 3 in the morning. Occasional barking is fine. We cannot expect our pup to be silent all the time. It is only when it starts to bark all the time that we need to do something about it. You certainly are not alone if you have this problem. It is one of the most common complaints many dog owners have. To make matters worse, this is a problem that can be difficult to solve. So, why do dogs bark?

Step 1: Why Dogs Bark

There are many reasons why your dog barks. Remember that barking is a natural form of communication, after all. The first step is to understand why your dog is barking before you can see to it that the problem is solved. Sometimes, the cause is quite obvious such as seeing a squirrel in the backyard. This kind of barking is intended to alert you to an intruder or noise. If you hear this kind of barking at 3 in the morning, then there may be something concerning (hopefully, there won't come a time when you hear it). Your dog may be barking to get your attention because it wants food or a cuddle. Whether your dog barks to alert you or to gain your attention, it will take some practice to make that habit go away. Until a better behavior is taught, your dog will bark when it receives the same stimulus. In some cases, your dog may just bark out of pure boredom. Then, the solution is very simple. Just give them more physical and mental stimulation and you should be good to go.

Step 2: Not Reward Barking

The only form of punishment in positive reinforcement training is not giving a reward. The same can be applied here by not rewarding your dog for barking. If you reward thrm, whether it is a treat or a simple pet, it will reinforce this behavior. In fact, even attention reinforcesthis behavior. If you go over to check what your dog is barking at, or you just shout at them, it is a form of reward too. To make matters worse, such behavior may worsen over time because your dog learns that barking gets a reaction. This is how you should approach the problem:

- If your dog is barking for attention, turn and walk away. Only give your dog what it wants when it is quiet.
- If your dog barks when it wants food, leave the kitchen. Return only when it has stopped.
- If your dog is barking to go outside, wait until it is quiet before opening the door. The exception is, of course, when it needs to "go".
- If your dog barks at someone walking by your house, don't call them until it is quiet.

Doing the above should be enough to stop your dog from barking for attention, especially if you reward your dog for doing the right thing instead. The only problem is that barking itself can be self-reinforcing. For instance, if your dog barks at the mailman to go away, the act of the postman leaving is perceived as a reward. This reinforces the barking even though you ignore your dog. In such situations and for most types of alert barking, you may need to instill an alternative behavior into your dog.

Step 3: Training an Alternative Behavior

After you have determined the reason your dog barks and eliminated the reward from them (if at all possible), the next step is to teach alternative behavior. First, listen for exactly when your dog barks. Does it start letting it rip as soon as it hears footsteps outside or does it wait until the person is right outside the door? The key here is to find your dog's tolerance level. Some dogs bark as soon as they see something. Others wait until it is close enough. Then, teach your dog that a different behavior gets a reward. So, interrupt the behavior before your dog reaches its barking threshold.

When your dog sees or hears the trigger and before it starts barking, ask them to perform a behavior that you want. You can ask them to sit, lie down, or just look at you. This will take its eyes off whatever it is that triggers them. When you've successfully interrupted them, give your dog a treat and a lot of praise. If you miss the trigger and your dog starts barking, don't interrupt them because that is rewarding your dog for barking. Instead, just ignore them and wait for the next opportunity. If possible, I recommend you have someone create the trigger so you can practice. Of course, you cannot always practice all the time as you cannot be with your dog constantly when someone walks by. This practice is great for noise triggers because your dog often hears people coming way before seeing them so repeat this process as often as possible. It is time-consuming, true, but your dog will eventually understand what you want them to do when faced with a certain trigger. Another thing to keep in mind is that your dog may bark with a hint of fear in its voice. Observe your dog's facial expression to determine its fear or anxiety threshold and interrupt its behavior before it gets too anxious. It would be too late already if your dog starts getting stressed or anxious.

Step 4: Preventing Reinforcement

The final step is to remove the trigger by keeping your dog away to avoid reinforcement whenever you cannot train your dog. This can mean keeping your dog inside with you as opposed to letting them run loose in the garden. It can be keeping them in a room at the back of the house whenever the postman comes. If you crate-trained your dog successfully, keeping your dog in the crate is a good option as well. You can also directly address the trigger by removing it to prevent barking from becoming a habit. If your dog has a habit of barking at people at the fence, then I suggest blocking their vision through the fence by building a higher fence.

What Not to Do

As always, there are common pitfalls that dog owners commit when they attempt to teach their dogs to stop barking at literally everything. One of which is shouting or physically hurting their dog. This is never a good solution to any unwanted behavior. Other than ruining the owner/pet relationship, such harsh methods will create negative associations. Even if your dog does not bark, it will be stressed and can become aggressive the next time it is in the same situation.

Preventing Biting

Knowing how to stop puppies from biting also requires patience from both the dog and the owner. Skipping this exercise may mean you end up with a chewed chair leg or a demolished sandal. While some owners may defend that dogs are just teething or this is just a method of understanding the world, chewing is nonetheless very annoying, especially when it results in the ruin of your perfectly good and expensive shoes.

It is true puppies use their teeth to explore the world in addition to their eyes, ears, and nose. They primarily use their mouth to play, explore, and teeth all the time. There is a good reason behind this behavior, but we need to first look at their teeth in more detail before we can seek to understand them.

Puppy Teeth

Puppies are born without teeth. At two to three weeks old, your dog will develop their milk teeth, which are called the incisors. Puppies normally have twelve incisors, six on the top and another six on the bottom. The four canine teeth start to show up only after four weeks, which are the four sharp and long teeth. Between three to six weeks, your dog should develop its pre-molars.

When your dog is about eight weeks old, it should have a complete set of milk teeth. There should be 28 in total, 14 up top and 14 down low:

- 12 incisors
- 4 canines
- 12 pre-molars

When your dog is about eight to twelve weeks old, their milk teeth should start to fall out because another set of adult teeth is growing and pushing the milk teeth out. Most puppies just swallow their milk teeth, but you may find some of them around your house. As you can probably guess, puppies do not have access to dental care like us so they have to suck it up. This phase is pretty painful for your pup, as you can imagine having to feel your teeth falling out without any anesthetic to help ease the pain. During this phase, I recommend you visit your vet to make sure that there is no infection and to see if your dog's adult teeth are forming properly, not to mention to check if your dog has a normal bite. The normal bite is also called a scissor bite because the upper incisors sit in front of the lower incisors when the mouth is closed. Certain breeds like pugs may have a reverse scissor bite where the lower incisors sit in front of the upper incisors instead due to the short muzzle. After all, the milk teeth have fallen out and the adult teeth set in, there should be 42 teeth in total:

- 12 incisors
- 4 canines
- 16 pre-molars
- 10 molars

You may notice the addition of 4 more pre-molars and 10 molars, which were nonexistent in puppies. Why is that? While puppies do not need molars, adult dogs need them to grind and crush bones, meat, your shoes, etc. The incisors are needed to rip meat off and scrape it off bones. The canines serve as a hook to puncture and capture prey.

With so many teeth, it is not a surprise to see why bite inhibition is so vital. Getting your skin punctured by the four canines is very nasty, but a nip caused by the incisors can be just as painful. It is not just the teeth that we need to be worried about, either. It is also the strength of the jaw that can do serious damage. Thankfully, puppies have weak jaws as they have not fully developed. It is ideal to train your dog to not bite anything before those jaws develop though.

Your dog's teeth are super sharp because they are carnivores. They need them for two main reasons: independence and bite inhibition. As I have said earlier, anyone who has been nipped by a puppy will understand how sharp their teeth are. With that in mind, let us consider what it feels like to be breastfeeding those puppies.

When those sharp teeth start to come through, the mother will become more and more irritated because of how painful it is to breastfeed them. Eventually, she will be reluctant to nurse them and want to move away from her puppies. This will force the puppies to look for an alternative food source. Those sharp teeth force the puppies to become independent, which is when the weaning phase starts. The puppies understand that they need to find other food sources if they want to survive.

The sharp teeth not only annoy their mother but also other dogs in the pack. This leads us into the second reason, bite inhibition. Puppies constantly play with their mouths. When they start to bite each other, they too will feel the pain and this often ended up with the bitten puppy retaliating or moving away from the biting puppy. This is when your puppy learns bite inhibition to understand social etiquette. Puppies generally learn this on their own when they play around with other puppies. However, if they are alone and only have you to play with, then they may not learn this valuable lesson.

Stopping Puppy Bites

The best way to stop your puppy from biting you is by doing exactly what a puppy would if it got bitten. Simply stop giving attention to your pup to deny themthe reward, and only give them that when it acts appropriately. From there, you can start to reinforce better alternatives. Here's how:

- Withdraw attention: Your puppy needs to learn that when it bites, it won't be getting the good things
- Positive reinforcement: When your puppy starts to play appropriately, continue playing with them, which is something that it wants.
- Provide alternative: Take the slipper away from the pup and give it its own rope chew or toy.

Of course, it is not always this simple. Stopping a puppy from biting may need a better understanding than what I have pointed out above. For instance, you may need a different approach if your pup has separation anxiety. You also need to understand bite inhibition, triggers, and types of biting.

Bite Inhibition

Think about the difference between punching someone playfully on the shoulder and punching someone in the face when they have wronged you. What is the difference other than the emotion? Force. Bite inhibition is simply learning how to limit the force and strength of your puppy's bite. It tells them that other dogs and humans are not as tough as the table leg it used to chew on. Because the only defense for a dog is biting, they need to learn bite inhibition to limit the damage a dog can do. Every dog can and will bite out of fear and anxiety.

When puppies play together, they will chew and nip on each other. However, when one takes it too far, they will hurt others. This is when you hear the loud yelp or squeal. It tells the offending puppy that it bit a little too hard. When this happens, the game usually ends, which means the denial of reward for the offending puppy. Through this trial and error, puppies learn that playtime is over when they bite hard. This is operant learning, which is when your dog learns its lesson the hard way.

So now we understand why learning bite inhibition at an early age is crucial. Dogs who learn how to use their mouth gently are less likely to bite hard and pierce the skin if they ever bite someone out of fear or anxiety.

As I have mentioned earlier, they naturally learn this as they grow up with a mother and sibling. But what if your pup is fed by your hands with a baby bottle and only have you to play with? As I have mentioned earlier, if your pup starts to nip or mouths at you during play, simply withdraw attention. Follow the three bullet points above and your pup should learn eventually.

Rough Play

Normally, I don't recommend playing rough with your pet because it is similar to biting hard. A little rough and tumble are fine but there is a line you should not cross. Unfortunately, children are the ones who often cross this line. This can cause your puppy to panic as it thinks it is being attacked, and retaliate, which can lead to a mess. As with any other training methods, teaching bite inhibition requires consistency. Everyone in the house needs to be teaching the dog the same thing.

As I said a little rough and tumble is fine but when there is contact between the dog's mouth and the skin or clothing, the game ends. The same goes for the tug of war I have described earlier. The message for your pup here is that lively and energetic play is acceptable. Being a little rough is fine. However, biting people or their clothing is not.

What Causes Puppies to Bite

All of us want to see our puppies running around in the dog park and playing and chasing other dogs but, through all of those interactions, your pup may develop aggressive tendencies. Indicators of aggressive intents when biting include a fixed gaze, stiff posture, and deep tone of growling. There are many reasons why puppies become aggressive. The most common reason is that it solves the problem. Such animalistic instinct is perfectly understandable because some of us turn to violence to get things done as well. Aggression can come from frustration, guarding (toys, food, etc.), anxiety, and the lack of appropriate socialization. Anxiety and frustration, in particular, can be a result of punishment.

There are a few biting types. Understanding and identifying them are important so you know what behavior you need to focus on during training. You can break down puppy biting into four categories:

- Exploration and play
- Aggressive
- Guarding
- Teething

All of these can be differentiated by your pup's body language. If your dog has that innocent and relaxed look on its face, then it is most likely exploring or playing. Aggressive and guarding bites, on the other hand, are accompanied by a stiff body, wrinkled face, snarling, growling, and the exposure of the teeth. This indicates a building tension and a bite could follow very soon.

Mouthing, Biting, and Nipping

All of these are completely normal behaviors in dogs. The only problem is that some pups have the tendency to do any of those excessively, which is why we need to teach them proper behavior, well into their adulthood if need be.

Nipping is light nibbling. It occurs regularly during play and exploration and your pup should project happiness and energy. Mouthing occurs during teething and can be easily seen when your puppy is gnawing on something. Biting is self-explanatory. It is displayed by aggressive dogs. Biting is a habit we want to control here as it can cause serious injury.

Some General Guidelines

You should take the time to allow your dog to socialize at a very young age so they can learn bite inhibition, making it easy for you to teach your dog restraint. Playtime is crucial for your pup as it learns social etiquette. Getting them to socialize with other puppies is the best approach because it learns from others what is and is not appropriate, both for play and using their teeth. Playing is a great opportunity because puppies love to play, so it is a great opportunity to teach restraint and other puppies are a better teacher in this regard. However, if your puppy is biting too hard or too much, you need to start teaching them at home to reinforce bite inhibition. Here are some general guidelines when you train your pup at home about bite inhibition:

- Stop playing immediately when your pup starts mouthing or biting. Deny them attention (reward) by turning away. After a few seconds, if your dog stops mouthing, you can continue playing with them.
- Say something like "Ow" when your dog bites you. When it stops, give them praise and affection.
- Use the command "gentle" when you give your dog treats and slowly roll out the treat in your hand to themif it is not biting or mouthing.
- Teach your puppy the "Off" command so you can get them to take their mouth away from your hand. Whenever it does that, give it a treat.
- Make sure to have some chew toys such as Kongs or Everlasting Treat Balls so your puppy can chew on those instead. I advise against using other toys such as soft squeakers or fabric toys because these actually teach your pup that it is acceptable to chew things up, which is counterintuitive.
- Do not clamp their mouth shut or hit them on the nose to punish your dog for biting. It can send your dog into a fight or flight stage and cause them to bite your hand instinctively.
- Do not tease your puppy or try to start playing with your hands.

Preventing Chewing

Almost all the dogs I have worked with love chewing, and this is also quite natural. However, when chewing leads to the destruction of objects in your house, it becomes a problem. That is why chew toys are created for your dog so it can chew on those instead of your expensive shoes. Chewing can be a recreational activity for your dog, but excessive and destructive chewing can be a sign of a deeper problem such as separation anxiety.

Chewing, in general, is a stress reliever for your dog and releases a hormone called endorphin in your dog, causing them to feel good. On the other hand, chewing on the frame of your door or window means that it is trying to get out, which is a behavioral problem. As with any behavioral issue, I recommend taking your dog to the vet to have it checked thoroughly to rule out any medical causes that could exacerbate the behavior. Other than that, here are some ways you can stop your dog from chewing:

- No matter what causes your dog to chew excessively, exercise and enrichment are key to changing the desire to chew in your dog. Your puppy is energetic, which means it is more likely to indulge in destructive behaviors to burn all of that energy. If it is tired, it would be a happy little pup and does not want to chew excessively.

- Create a dog-proof room (or dog-proof your entire house) or use baby gates to keep your dog in a certain area where you know it cannot cause destruction by chewing when you leave it unsupervised. Just make sure this room in your house is close to the busy areas so your dog does not feel isolated.

- Give your dog appropriate chew toys to keep them busy. Just make sure that they are durable and safe for your dog even with heavy chewing.

- Find a good outlet for your dog's energy. Taking your dog out for a walk gives them the physical exercise he needs, but it also needs something to work its mind. Play some games with them as I have described above, or give them puzzles or interactive toys to play with.

- If possible, find a sport in which both you and your dog love to do together to release any pent up stress or tension your pup may be feeling.

Preventing Digging

As with any other bad behavior, we need to understand why dogs dig before we can address this problem. As always, there are many reasons why your puppy digs. But when it digs without actually going to the bathroom, it could be boredom. It isn't as damaging when it does it in the house, but no one wants to dislocate their ankle when they trip over a hole created a few hours ago. If your dog has a habit of digging up your entire yard, I recommend you study the day to day schedule of your pup and restructure the whole thing. Other than that, dogs are known to dig to escape the heat. The ground beneath the surface is cooler, so they dig it up and sleep in the pit on a hot day. Another common reason is that your pup may be curious. For instance, if your pup notices that you are digging in the yard, whether to garden or landscape, they will be curious and want to investigate what you are working on. If it sees that you dig a hole and refill it, they will automatically assume that you bury something good under there. Because curiosity is a great motivator for your pup, it will literally unearth everything in the name of science. If it believes that freedom is on the other side of the fence, it will dig underneath it. If it thinks that you are hiding something under your precious flower bed, well, it will not leave a flower standing. To make matters worse, just like barking, digging is self-reinforcing because it is a fun activity for your dog. This means getting your dog to stop digging is going to be a very difficult task.

If your dog digs excessively, then there is probably an environmental factor that motivates your dog to dig. It can be boredom, or it can be the heat. Again, there can be many factors that lead to this behavior. The lack of training is also one of them. Thankfully, there are ten actionable steps you can follow to stop your dog from digging. These are the most effective practices in the dog training world. If you follow every single one of them, your dog should understand that digging is a big no-no.

Give Them a Proper Digging Spot

Similar to potty training, the best way to get your dog to stop digging all over the place is by giving them their own digging spot. As I have said earlier, digging is a self-reinforcing behavior, so it is unrealistic to assume that your dog will one day stop digging. Your pup will continue to do that for the rest of its life, so it is better to just embrace its flaws and at least control where it should do it to minimize the damage done to your yard.

The digging site can be as simple as a kiddie pool or a boxed off area filled with sand or loose dirt. It can even be a specific space in your yard. Stick with what works best for you. If your pup ignores the sandbox you set up for them and goes for the spot underneath the tree, then use the latter as the designated excavation site for your pup.

Remember that curiosity is a powerful motivator for your pup? You can use that to your advantage by burying chew bone or toys in that area. I suggest making sure your dog sees you burying it to pique its interest and get it to come and investigate. It will quickly come around, sniff and dig up. This is a perfect strategy for two reasons. First, digging reinforces its behavior, but it rewards them again by giving them toys. It will eventually come around to the exact same spot to dig because it knows that it will find something interesting in there.

Positive Reinforcement Training

You can further capitalize on double reinforcement by giving your pup praise and some treats when your dog digs in the designated digging spot. Normally, I recommend rewarding sparingly with treats, but you shouldn't skimp on the treats in this training. The positive reinforcement you give is going to increase your dog's desire to dig exclusively in the spot you gave them. It does not help if your dog digs in its designated area, but also everywhere else to check if there are any goodies to be found. So, you want to convince your dog that this is literally the best spot for him as soon as possible.

Do Not Get Angry

I, for one, always get upset when my dog digs up my pristine backyard. I understand that it can be really hard to not become angry at your pup when it does something that you know it understands it is not supposed to do.

It seems that your pup is taking a defiance stance against you, which can be irritating after all the things you have given them such as food, shelter, etc. In some cases, it is defiance. Most of the time though, it is just boredom or a plea for attention and affection.

No matter what the reason is, it is crucial that you do not show anger or aggression toward your pup over the problem. Doing so will only ruin the relationship you have been trying to establish so far. Instead, be firm and commanding when you confront such behavior, without being violent or imposing.

When you approach your pup without showing any signs of threats, it will respond in kind. However, if your dog thinks you are going to hurt them, they may either flee or bite back. If it is the latter, you can be sure that they will draw first blood.

Tire Your Dog Out

Your dog would prefer to be sleeping than digging if it is exhausted. If your schedule lacks mental and physical stimulation, consider adding them in so your dog gets enough exercise. By the time it's through with the activities, it won't have any strength left to go digging. However, certain dogs are more energetic than others so yours may need a lot more exercise to avoid boredom. If your pup gets bored, then they will indulge in destructive behaviors. Digging is, of course, one of them.

Crate Train

I highly recommend crate training your pup because it will not dig up its own den. If your pup digs excessively and you cannot keep an eye on them all the time, consider putting them in their own crate as it will stop them from being anxious and prevent boredom-induced digging binges. Of course, that does not mean that theywill suddenly become excited. They still need an outlet for their energy, so consider throwing in a few toys it can play with when you are away.

Do Not Leave Dogs Unsupervised

Most dogs, even those that like to exercise a lot, do not like it if you leave them outside alone for hours. They will get bored and stressed by external environmental factors such as other dog's barks. When this happens, your dog will start digging to cope.

Fill the Hole with Waste

This is going to be disgusting if you are not used to handling dog's waste, but at least it is one of the most effective ways to quell your dog's digging behavior if it fancies a spot where you don't want them to dig. You can fill all the problem spots with your dog's waste and your dog will not dig there instantly. Just like us, dogs are a clean animal and they do not want to mess with their own waste unless they have to.

You can take it a step further by mixing the waste with water and then water the area you don't want your dog to dig with the feces concoction you just mixed up. Of course, it will make your yard stinky for about a week at most, but your dog is going to smell it for much longer and avoid the area.

Give Your Dog Bonus

At a certain point, you will have to leave your dog unsupervised for an extended period of time. When you do, make sure you reward your dog for waiting for you by keeping them busy while you are away. A large bone or puzzle toy should be enough to keep them occupied.

Give Your Dog a Pool

As I have mentioned earlier, dogs sometimes dig to create a hole in which they rest in to escape the heat. German Shepherds are one of those breeds that do not have a high tolerance for heat. But you can provide your pup with a better alternative – a pool. Consider digging a half-full kiddie pool for your dog so they can hop in to chill. It can be any container as long as it is big enough.

Use Plastic Cover Wire Netting

To protect your flower beds or other precious plants, consider getting one of this at the local garden store or plant nursery. It is a great solution to keeping your dog off the plants and keeping the weeds down as well.

Dealing with Separation Anxiety

Separation anxiety plays out in many ways. Your dog may scratch at the door, cry, whine, or bark excessively. They may go to the bathroom in the house or chew on everything they can get their paws on. How can you tell it is a product of separation anxiety? Simple. It happens whenever you leave the house. Other problems such as chewing, digging, barking may occur whether you are present or not. The distinction here is presence.

There are many reasons why puppies develop separation anxiety and we still do not fully understand it. Whatever the case may be, it is crucial to realize that the destructive tendency caused by this anxiety is not malicious. It is believed that such behaviors result from panic or simply serve as a coping behavior, which is totally understandable. Many people turn to alcohol and even drugs to cope with problems, so what your dog does is not so different. Therefore, punishing your puppy for what they did will not solve the problem, it may even make it worse. The best approach would be adjusting your puppy to being alone.

You can help your pup learn to be comfortable being alone by taking a little time and following the pointers below. Start as soon as possible after you get your new puppy. It may already be too late if your dog develops separation anxiety. By then, you may need to consult a professional.

- Have a specific routine and stick to it. Unlike us, puppies like routine. So, create a schedule for your puppy and make sure everyone, including you and everyone else in the house, stick to it.
- Practice preventative training.
- Make sure your puppy take care of its business before you crate it. They cannot hold it in for that long and forcing them to stay in close proximity to its own feces will only stress them more.
- Crate them for short periods of time when you are around. For instance, if you are watching television, when you are reading or watching TV, put your puppy in its crate and put the crate close to you. Increase the crate time gradually and reward it if it remains calm by giving calm praise.
- From there, start leaving your puppy in its crate and go somewhere out of sight. Leave them in their crate unsupervised for a few minutes at a time and then gradually increase the time inside the crate.
- Try to limit the attention your dog gets, and the time it takes you to prepare to leave. Make your exit low-key if possible. That way, the act of you leaving would not be such a shock to your pup. It may even think that your departure is normal.
- When you finally let your puppy out of the crate, remain calm and try not to overdo your greeting. A little pat should suffice. You don't want to excite them.
- I advise against crating dogs all the time, but that does not mean you should give your puppy the whole house to play with. Do not rush freedom. Normally, puppies are not supposed to be left unsupervised until they are at least a year-and-a-half (18 months) or older.
- Try to make sure that there is at least someone in the house. If not possible, consider hiring a puppy walker or ask your neighbor to visit them during the day while everyone else is out at work or in school. Make sure that your dog has some company.
- If possible, keep your schedule similar on weekends so your puppy does not get confused when everyone is gone on Monday.

Other Tips

Many puppies whine or cry when you leave them alone for extended periods of time. This is normal behavior. Real separation anxiety is defined as destructive or disruptive behavior by a puppy such as destroying the room, constant barking and whiling, or inappropriate elimination in his crate or on the carpet, even though you have potty trained them properly. If you cannot resolve this problem on your own, I recommend you seek out professional help.

Other than that, whenever you leave the house, make it uneventful. By making your departure overly emotional with lots of hugs and goodbyes, you may end up increasing your puppy's anxiety level. You can give them an interactive toy to keep them occupied while you are gone.

Finally, do not get too excited when you return. Let your puppy out of the crate and take them outside so they can eliminate. As they get older, they can hold it in for much longer so you can wait until they are calm and quiet. Then, you can let them out, greet, and praise them for being calm and quiet.

Scheduling

Just like us, dogs are a creature of habit. They need a routine to follow and it is better if you decide what they should do. If you give them a free run of their own time, you may not like what they choose to do with so much time. Then again, the same can be said for us.

Anyway, schedules are very crucial for your puppy. You need to have a precise feeding, exercise, and potty time. Creating a schedule should also involve everyone in the house so everyone is involved in caring for the puppy, not to mention making every day consistent for your pup, which is something you should always strive for.

Other than being a creature of habit, having a precise schedule makes your puppy happy because it knows what to expect at a certain point in time, giving thema sense of security. It also keeps everyone on the same page as far as who is responsible for each task. Scheduling your puppy's activities also makes it easier for you to train and control your puppy. Having a schedule is especially useful if you are housetraining your puppy.

Scheduling Food

Make sure that everyone in the house feeds your puppy precisely the sameamount of food, feeding time, the way of feeding, and the place where your puppy eats. On the package, you should see an instruction on how to feed your dog. Follow that instruction and make sure that there is water available for your dog. After that, it is a good idea to take your dog out to eliminate if you plan to crate them soon after meal time.

If you know exactly when your dog eats and drinks, you should have a good idea when it needs to go outside to take care of its business. You also get to train its digestive system to adapt to the schedule, which is extremely helpful when you are housetraining them.

Potty Scheduling

As I have mentioned earlier, it is best to think ahead, especially when you plan when your puppy should eliminate. Take your puppy outside when you see the first sign that it needs to go to the bathroom rather than wait for too long and run the risk of them accidentally soiling inside your house.

If you are precise about their feeding and drinking time, then your pup should also have a predictable time when it needs to hit the bathroom. The more you get them to do it outside, the less likely it will be for them to have an accident indoors. At the early phase of their potty training, make sure to keep an eye on them in case it wanders off and causes an accident in the house. You want to be able to respond immediately at the first sign that it needs to hit the bathroom. If an accident occurs in the house, just make sure to dispose of the waste and clean the area thoroughly with an odor neutralizing cleaner so your dog does not cause an accident in the same place again.

As always, do not scold or punish your puppy after an accident. If your puppy wants to go inside the house, clap loudly or say "no" and take them outside quickly and reward them after. In reality, dogs want to make you happy and you can show them how to do it. The clearer you show to them that it needs to do its business outside, the quicker it catches on to the idea.

Puppies need to eliminate frequently, especially for smaller breeds. At about eight weeks old, they need to go out about every few hours during the day. When they are four months old, they can hold it in for about four to five hours. Most puppies can hold it in through the entire night when they are about four months old. At about nine months old, three or four trips outside is enough, although it does not hurt to let them eliminate outside more frequently.

Scheduling Exercise and Play

Exercise is one of the most important things for a puppy with regards to health. It is beneficial for you as well in the sense that your pup won't use the extra energy to pursue destructive behaviors. Lack of appropriate exercise can cause puppies to exhibit excessive chewing or other destructive behaviors because they become bored or try to burn off extra energy. When you continue to neglect them, they may become overweight due to overfeeding and lack of exercise program. So, take some time to walk your puppy to get in some exercise for both you and your dog. Plus, they can use this opportunity to socialize with other humans and dogs. You can also use this opportunity to strengthen your bond while doing something together.

Chapter 11: Using a Clicker

We mentioned at the start that using a clicker has its downsides just like positive reinforcement, although the latter can be easily mitigated. In some cases, using positive reinforcement is not enough to teach your pup new behaviors or tricks. It may warrant the use of a clicker.

One downside of positive reinforcement is that the timing can be a bit off and you want to tell your dog the exact moment when it did something right. This is where clicker training comes in. It is yet another form of training that falls under positive reinforcement because it marks and rewards desirable behaviors. To do this, the trainer uses a clicker. It is a mechanical device that creates a short and distinct click to tell your pup exactly when it gets something right. Some argue that it is more effective than positive reinforcements through treats or affection. In general, positive reinforcement is effective, safe, and human way to teach your dog. The downside is dependence on the clicker. Your pup will not perform any command unless it can see the clicker because it perceives the clicker as the hand signal cue.

How is Clicker Training Effective?

Clicker training employs what researchers call operant conditioning, which is how animals intentionally perform a behavior to yield a desirable consequence, as clicker trained animals do.

Animals and people alike associate an action, event, place, person, object, based on experience or consequence, pleasant or not. The stronger the experience or consequence is tied to a certain event or environment, the stronger the association. This type of learning is called classical conditioning. It represents reflexive, automatic, or reactive behavior, not intentional behavior. Think of children. They may be fascinated by its color, but and want to touch it. They associate fire with beauty, which is a positive experience. So, they are tempted to touch it. When they do, they get burned and never want to be anywhere near the fire again. The experience associated with fire is then negative. The same can be said for animals. If you decide to punish your dog by putting them in a crate, they will associate that crate with social isolation and will do everything in their power to get out of there. This is classical conditioning.

Eventually, animals and humans start to learn to follow certain behaviors intentionally to get a reward or positive experience. This is operant conditioning. Clicker initially relies on classical conditioning, but it moves toward operant conditioning when your pup intentionally repeats the action to get a reward. Operant conditioning leads to purposeful behavior whereas classical conditioning creates habits.

We want dogs to learn through operant conditioning because the benefit is vast if it learns with purpose rather than by habit. One benefit is that your dog is willing to learn new behaviors. It would still remember its training years after because it was aware of it when it learned it. It did not pick up this behavior without being aware of it. Your pup will develop confidence in itself because it knows it has control over the consequences of its actions. They will be enthusiastic because it expects those consequences to be good.

Why is a Clicker Used?

The main difference between clicker training and other reward-based training is accuracy, which means that the animal is told exactly which behavior gave them a reward. They know this from the distinct and unique clicks that happen at the exact moment as the desired behavior is performed. The reward then follows.

As you can probably tell, the clicker requires precise timing. Without hearing the click during the action, your dog may not associate the reward with the action. If you click late, your dog may even associate the reward with another, unpleasant behavior. With the clicker, you can precisely mark behaviors with the click so that your dog knows what it got right. This is why, for dog trainers, we call the click an "event marker". We sometimes call it a "bridging signal" as well because it connects the behavior to the reward.

Why Click is a Cue

Based on a previous chapter, you may be wondering what is the difference between the click and just a word? The former is a better alternative because the click is much clearer than speech. For one, the click is not usually heard in any other circumstances. If you take your dog out to the mall, it will hear many things, some of which may sound close to your verbal cue which will confuse them. On the other hand, the click means one thing only: a reward is coming because of what the dog did when it heard the click. It can be produced instantly and at the exact moment when the desired behavior occurs, no matter how subtle the behavior is. It can all be marked with a click.

Moreover, the click is unique. There are many ways to say "sit" based on intonation. This can confuse your pup as well. On the other hand, the click sounds the same all the time. So, its meaning remains constant. As I have mentioned earlier, we have many ways to communicate. Dogs, however, communicate mainly through body language. It is difficult for them to discern a single word out of all the stream of meaningless words they hear people speak every day. The click always stands out and your pup knows it is directed at them, and it always brings good news.

This clarity of the click is effective as it allows trainers to communicate properly with their animals. The level of interactions can see an increase based on the clicks and the training sessions become more interesting and fun for all parties involved.

How Does the Clicker Training Work?

It is simple. You click the moment the behavior occurs. When your pup sits, you click. Think of clicking as taking a photo. You take a snapshot of the activities you want as it happens.

How Do Clicker Trainers Ask for Behaviors?

Unlike any other traditional training method, clicker training works by getting the pup to understand the behavior first before introducing the command or cue. Cue is basically the name of the behavior such as "stay", or a simple hand gesture. In fact, any clear signal can be used as a cue. Until your pup learns the behavior, giving it a name is meaningless.

When your pup has been clicked many times for behavior and repeats the behavior several times confidently knowing that it knows exactly what earns it a click and a reward, it is ready to learn the name of the behavior. This is when you introduce the cue.

To introduce the cue, you say the command or signal the cue before the animal performs the behavior. After several repetitions, you can click and reward your pup when it does the behavior, but only when you give it the cue. Do not click or reward them if it performs the behavior without the cue. Then, your pup learns that it needs to listen or watch for the cue. It knows that if it does this behavior now, it will get a click and then a reward.

What if My Pup Fails to Obey the Cue?

Dogs that have been clicker trained want to perform behaviors that they have been rewarded for in the past. If they understand the meaning of the cue clearly and want the reward, they will perform the behavior. If they fail to perform the behavior, it is not that they are disobeying. There can be many reasons. You can diagnose the problem by asking the following questions:

1. Does my dog know the meaning of the cue?
2. Does my dog know the meaning of the cue in the environment in which it was first taught? If yes, then does it knows it in the environment in which it was given?
3. Is the reward for performing the behavior enticing enough for my dog?

After answering those questions, you should be able to find out the root cause and change the training process to ensure that your pup understands the meaning of the cue in all environments, despite the distractions, and feels that the reward for the behavior is sufficient.

Why Not Use Punishments as well as Rewards?

The argument goes like this: The consequence of any behavior can be both pleasant and unpleasant, so why shouldn't punishments follow unwanted behaviors? Why should we only reward wanted behaviors?

Many studies show that punishments can decrease the frequency of unwanted behavior, but often end up creating another unwanted behavior in addition to causing anxiety and fear in your pup. So, the result of training through punishment is always unpredictable and hard to control.

Plus, punishment is not always identified with an event marker. It always comes after an undesirable behavior and is rarely connected with specific behavior. For your pup, it sees the punishment as a random and meaningless event. Therefore, punishment is less effective compared to the combined use of event markers and positive reinforcement.

Clicker training also reinforces the relationship between the owner and the animal as the training itself focus more on rewards and positive experience rather than negative. Just like the difference between operant conditioning and classical conditioning, the difference is the attitude and enthusiasm in your pup. It is willing to work to earn rewards, not to avoid punishment. The difference is vast.

Clicker Training and Negative Behaviors

As I have said at the start of the book, any form of positive reinforcement training is not so effective in getting rid of behavior in the sense that it takes a long time. Still, the upside of not hurting your dog physically and psychologically makes it the ideal approach to dog training.

Getting rid of negative behaviors requires some form of punishment, but in this case, we use the lack of reward as the punishment. To get rid of unwanted behavior, we just need to avoid reinforcing it. If a behavior is not rewarding to your pup, it will stop doing it eventually. If it persists, there may be an underlying reason that reinforces its negative behavior. In some cases, such as excessive barking and digging, the behavior itself is self-reinforcing. For instance, digging is fun for your dog because it is a form of exercise and exploration, so digging is a reward in itself.

To correct this behavior, you need to give your dog an alternative desirable behavior to replace the unwanted one. Using our previous example, one solution is to give them a designated digging spot. Studying the underlying problem is key. In some cases, your dog is just bored, so provide them with extra activities. Maybe it just needs longer to sleep.

Do Clicker and Treats Need to Be Used Forever?

This is a common question among dog owners when they hear about our methods of dog training. I mentioned that the reward needs to be worthwhile for the pup to perform the behavior, but this is only during the training process. When your dog learns the behavior and its cue, you normally do not need to click because it already understands the behavior. You still need to reward your pup, of course. But over time, you can replace treats with something less intensive such as praise or a pat, and you can reward intermittently. You can also reward learned cue and behavior by real-life rewards. For instance, if your dog learns to sit quietly at the door without scratching or barking to get out, the reward then is you opening the door to let them out. You only need to use the clicker and treats for when you want to teach your dog new behaviors.

How to Do It

To start training your dog using clicker training, you will need a clicker. It is a device that makes a distinct clicking sound when pressed. You can find it in pet stores and it comes in various shapes and colors. The click is much faster and convenient than saying "Good boy/girl!", so you can precisely mark the behavior you want to reinforce. Just make sure you get the timing right! Before we begin, I want to discuss the basics first:

- First, find a quiet place, free from distractions before you begin.
- Keep training sessions short so your up does not become tired or bored. Three five-minutes sessions throughout the day are much more efficient than one fifteen-minute session a day.
- Break a behavior or trick down into small steps, and progress from a learning step to the next step until the entire behavior is completely learned.
- Train only one behavior at a time until it is learned. Then, move on to the next.

Click and Treat

At the start of the training phase, you need to establish the association between the click and the treat that follows. When your dog is calm, click the clicker and give them a treat immediately. Do this about ten times until your dog looks up at you when he hears the click. When that happens, you know that he has come to associate the click with the treat. At the start, your dog may be startled by the sound of the clicker as it is the sort of sound that it has not heard before. If so, hide the clicker in your pocket or suppress the sound using a towel. It should get used to the click eventually.

Starting Lessons

There is no particular order to the behaviors your dog can learn via clicker training. If your dog has no previous training, I suggest you start with the sit command. Make sure you have the clicker and some treats.

First, touch the treat to your dog's nose to grab his attention. It should follow the treat as you move your hand higher and toward his eyes. Your dog's rear should hit the ground as you do this. The moment it happens, click and give them the treat.

Repeat this process several times. Then, put the treat to their nose briefly before taking it away. Your dog may assume that it needs to sit in order to get the treat. If it does, click and treat. It is fine if it gets up immediately after. We want to mark its sits with clicks, and your dog will remember what it was doing that causes the click. If your pup barks, mouths at your hand, or jumps up to get the treat, take the treat away, ignore them, wait a moment, and then try again. There is no need to give the command "Sit". We want them to understand that whenever it sits, it hears the click, and the treat follows.

When your pup makes the connection between the behavior and the click, you can try to stretch out the time between the time it sits, the click, then the treat. Start by extending out the delay between those three events, but do not wait for too long. You want to see your dog looks at you expectantly. When it does, click and give them a treat. If it gets up, ignore them and try again after a while. Eventually, they should develop a habit of coming up to you and sit down so they can get their click and treat.

Attaching Command

When your dog learns to sit reliably, this is the time to attach the command. Using the previous example, say "Sit" or give a clear signal just as he starts to lower his rear, and before you click and treat. Say the command once ("Sit", not "Sit, sit, sit") as you move the treat over its head until it understands that it needs to sit when it hears you say "Sit".

As I have said before, you should only attach the command to the behavior only after you have your dog execute the command. A meaningless word to your dog may start to make sense for them when it is paired with an action over many repetitions. First, have your dog perform the behavior regularly. Then, attach a name to it, and take away the click and treat as it becomes more proficient. Finally, phase out the click and treat.

Eventually, you want to reward them intermittently. This is known as variable positive reinforcement. You want to make sure that your dog responds even when you do not have treats in hand. Keep practicing regularly and be consistent with the command until it is firmly established. The end result is your dog sitting when you say "Sit", and the reward is a simple pat or praise.

You can then move on to another behavior or command, following the same process. The possibility is endless when it comes to teaching your dog.

Erasing Negative Behaviors

Clicker training follows the same principle as positive reinforcement in the sense that the dog gets rewarded for the desired behavior. There will come a time when you want to let your dog know if it does something wrong. You can use the "No" command from chapter 5, or use the "Wrong" command. For instance, if you are teaching your dog to sit, and it jumps in an attempt to snatch the treat out of your hand, say "Wrong" calmly, withdraw the treat, and ignore them until it settles down. Do NOT use the clicker to mark wrongful behavior because it will expect you to give it a treat after the click. It should only be used to mark the desired behavior. After ignoring your dog for a while, try again. Do not yell, become frustrated, or jerk the treat away. Be consistent with the "Wrong" command as your dog eventually understands that it means it did something he shouldn't do. Do this with every behavior you are trying to teach.

Focus on the behavior you want them to perform. If your dog jumps up, turn away from them and remain still. Do not move, talk, yell, push your dog down, or make eye contact with them. Watch them from the corner of your eyes until it calms down and puts all four paws on the floor. When it does that, click and give them a treat with petting and attention. If it jumps again, repeat the process.

Conclusion

Dog training does not have to be a tedious activity. It can be something that you can enjoy that ultimately leads to a well-behaved dog that you can take anywhere.

In this book, we have discussed some of the main behaviors necessary for your dog to live inside the house. Things such as training methods, positive reinforcements, discipline, crate training, house training, and fundamental commands.

As we have mentioned earlier, there are several training methods and they work best in certain circumstances. However, I highly recommend that you use positive reinforcement (and the clicker if necessary) as it creates a positive experience for your pup without traumatizing or hurting them physically.For the training regimen, as I have highlighted throughout the book, the most severe form of punishment is a firm "no" or not rewarding your pup whether it is giving them the treat or attention. Never hit, shout, or make loud noises at them as it will scare them.

Using positive reinforcement as a base, you can go on to teach your dog crate training by getting them to associate the crate as a safe haven. They should see it as a place where they can have some privacy. As mentioned earlier, the best option for an in-house crate is a metal crate. Have a plastic one when you need to transport your pooch around. Size-wise, make sure that the crate is large enough so that your pup can stand up, turn around, and lie down, but not large enough that he can soil one corner and sleep at the other.

Speaking of soiling, house training is intended to tell your dog where it can do its business. The start will be slow and tedious, but your pup should learn where his usual spot eventually so it can go there on his own. Learning how your dog is telling you when it needs to go is also crucial such as scratching at the door, pacing in circles, etc.

We went over five fundamental commands that help you establish many other commands and behaviors. Those five are sit, down, come, stay, and no. From there, you can proceed to teach your dog to fetch, follow, etc.

As you have already guessed, all of the above training have a certain pattern: consistency. This is the one thing I want you to take away from the book. If anything, keep in mind that any training is only successful when you are consistent with how you teach your dog. If you use a verbal cue, make sure you say the exact same thing each time (including pitch and pace). This is one of the main reasons why dogs do not obey commands. They can understand one word when spoken in a certain way, but not the other.

With all that said and done, thank you for reading this far. You deserve a treat yourself for putting so much effort into learning how to train your dog! With what I have revealed to you, you are equipped to train your puppy right at home with little fuss.

Other than that, I also have a personal message for you. The entire book is built on compassion for animals. I love animals, dogs especially, which motivates me to become a dog trainer. Many dogs are fortunate enough to have considerate owners. Some others are not. Some puppies are given up at a very young age, helpless in this cruel world. They need a place to call home and it is up to us to provide shelter. The animal shelter can only do so much. Whenever you want a new dog in the house, adopt. Don't buy. It is sweet to have an expensive pup at home, but it is a lot sweeter knowing that you have saved a pup from a harsh life and given them a place they can call home. Let's be honest here. No matter what breed or size the dog is, they are all good. With a little training, time, patience, and consistency, you can effectively teach your dog all the right behaviors.

Resources

If you are interested in learning more about dog training, I have compiled a list of links you can follow:

Chapter 1

- Dog behavior. (2019, June 15). Retrieved from https://en.wikipedia.org/wiki/Dog_behavior
- 7 Most Popular Dog Training Methods. (2019, January 10). Retrieved from https://dogtime.com/reference/dog-training/50743-7-popular-dog-training-methods

Chapter 2

- InsideDogsWorld. (2018, December 27). 15 Essential Commands to Teach Your Dog. Retrieved from https://www.insidedogsworld.com/essential-commands-to-teach-your-dog/
- 10 Frequently Asked Questions About Puppies. (n.d.). Retrieved from http://www.vetstreet.com/our-pet-experts/answers-to-10-of-the-most-common-questions-people-have-about-owning-a-new-puppy
- Puppy Training FAQ - Ultimate Puppy. (n.d.). Retrieved from https://www.ultimatepuppy.com/puppy-training-faq/ | https://www.fidosavvy.com/puppy-faqs.html

Chapter 3

- The 7 Most Important Dog Training Skills. (2019, April 15). Retrieved from https://www.rover.com/blog/important-dog-training-skills/
- Crate training 101. (n.d.). Retrieved from https://www.humanesociety.org/resources/crate-training-101
- Crate Training Your Puppy: The Key To A Pee-Free Home. (2017, April 3). Retrieved from https://www.caninejournal.com/crate-training-puppy/
- How To Crate Train Your Dog » PAWS. (n.d.). Retrieved from https://www.paws.org/library/dogs/training/how-to-crate-train-your-dog/

Chapter 4

- Admin. (2019, June 13). Tips for Potty Training Your New Puppy | Hill's Pet. Retrieved from https://www.hillspet.com/dog-care/training/puppy-potty-training-tips
- Tips for Housetraining Your Puppy. (2009, December 16). Retrieved from https://pets.webmd.com/dogs/guide/house-training-your-puppy#1

Chapter 5

- 5 Essential Commands You Can Teach Your Dog. (2018, September 23). Retrieved from https://www.cesarsway.com/dog-training/obedience/5-essential-commands-you-can-teach-your-dog

- 5 Simple Commands You Should Teach Your Puppy. (n.d.). Retrieved from https://www.akc.org/expert-advice/training/teach-your-puppy-these-5-basic-commands/
- Dr. Natalie Waggener. (n.d.). Five Basic Obedience Commands Your Dog Should Learn. Retrieved from https://www.southbostonanimalhospital.com/blog/five-basic-obedience-commands-your-dog-should-learn

Chapter 6

- 5 Dog Training Fundamentals For Every Dog. (2018, July 27). Retrieved from https://www.guthriepet.net/blog/dog-training-fundamentals/
- The Do's And Don'ts Of Positive Reinforcement. (2015, June 18). Retrieved from https://www.cesarsway.com/the-dos-and-donts-of-positive-reinforcement/

Chapter 7

- 7 Ways to Make Training Part of Everyday Life with Your Dog. (n.d.). Retrieved from https://www.petsafe.net/learn/7-ways-to-make-training-part-of-everyday-life-with-your-dog
- 7 Ways to Train Your Dog Every Day. (2015, November 9). Retrieved from https://www.thehonestkitchen.com/blog/7-plus-ways-to-train-your-dog-every-day/
- Jason Nicholas, BVetMed (. (n.d.). Simple Dog Training Tips For Your Daily Routine - Sit & Stay. Retrieved from https://www.preventivevet.com/dogs/simple-dog-training-tips-for-your-your-daily-routine-sit-and-stay

Chapter 8

- Adding Verbal Cues to Hand Signals. (2018, June 26). Retrieved from https://positivepartnersdogtraining.com/adding-verbal-cues-to-hand-signals/
- Stilwell, V. (2018, October 12). Teach Your Dog to Respond to Cues? Successfully. Retrieved from https://www.dogster.com/dog-training/teach-your-dog-to-respond-to-cues-successfully

Chapter 9

- 10 Simple and Fun Indoor Games For Your Dog. (n.d.). Retrieved from https://positively.com/contributors/10-simple-and-fun-indoor-games-for-your-dog/
- Dog Games. (n.d.). Retrieved from https://positively.com/dog-wellness/dog-enrichment/dog-games/
- Training Games for Puppy Classes. (2016, March 28). Retrieved from https://www.themoderndogtrainer.net/5-training-games-puppy-classes/

Chapter 10

- Stop Your Dog's Chewing. (n.d.). Retrieved from https://positively.com/dog-behavior/nuisance-behaviors/chewing/

- Hellopebby. (2019, May 23). How to Prevent Barking With Positive Reinforcement. Retrieved from https://www.getpebby.com/blog/how-to-prevent-barking-with-positive-reinforcement/

- How To Deal With Puppy Separation Anxiety. (2018, October 3). Retrieved from https://www.purina.com/articles/puppy/behavior/how-to-deal-with-puppy-separation-anxiety

- How to Stop a Puppy from Biting: 3 Fast & Easy Steps – All Things Dogs. (n.d.). Retrieved from https://www.allthingsdogs.com/how-to-stop-a-puppy-from-biting/

- Ouch, My Puppy is Biting Me! The Importance of Attending Puppy Class to Teach Bite Inhibition and Play Skills. (n.d.). Retrieved from https://positively.com/contributors/ouch-my-puppy-is-biting-me-the-importance-of-attending-puppy-class-to-teach-bite-inhibition-and-play-skills/

- Stop Dog From Digging: 10 Actionable Steps To Follow – DogsPie. (n.d.). Retrieved from https://www.dogspie.com/stop-dog-from-digging/

Chapter 11

- Clicker Training Positive Reinforcement. (n.d.). Retrieved from http://www.animalsguru.com/clicker-training.html

- Karen Pryor Clicker Training | The Leader in Positive Reinforcement Training. (n.d.). Retrieved from https://www.clickertraining.com/

- What Is Clicker Training? (n.d.). Retrieved from https://www.clickertraining.com/what_is_clicker_training

Positive Dog Training for Beginners 101

The Complete Practical Step by Step Guide to Training your Dog using Proven Modern Methods that are Friendly and Loving and Won't Cause your Dog Harm or Suffering

By
Matthew Hargreaves

Table of Contents

Introduction

Dogs are our best friend. However, because they don't speak our language, it is hard for us to understand why they behave a certain way. Your dog certainly wants to make you happy but doesn't know how. You want your dog to be a good boy as well, but he just does all the wrong things. Clearly, there is a miscommunication problem here.

Hello, I'm Matthew Hargreaves. I'm a passionate dog trainer and I have been working with these adorable four-legged canines since I can remember. My parents are avid animal lovers and we have all sorts of animals in our home. But I want to focus on dogs in this book because they are the easiest to raise and train.

As I've said earlier, the problem is that we do not understand dogs. If your dog displays various negative behaviors, then this book is for you. I want to help all dog owners train their dogs using proven modern methods that are both engaging and stress-free for your dog. What you want to do is train your dog using positive reinforcement, relationship-based training, as well as clicker training if necessary.

I am an advocate for positive reinforcement training as this has proven to be the most effective training method out there. I speak from my decades of experience in the dog training field and that of other dog trainers as well as many scientific studies on dogs' behaviors. Positive training will yield a well-trained and happy dog that loves the training process.

I will show you exactly why positive reinforcement training works and how you can do this right at home. I've broken everything down into an easy step-by-step tutorial so you can follow along easily. The training regimen I highlight in this book uses engaging and stress-free methods that both you and your dog can enjoy.

Remember, every day that you are not training your dog is another day that you have to put up with his poor behavior. You may have heard the saying, "You can't teach an old dog new tricks." In a way, another day that you put off training your dog means you lose another day of the narrow window opportunity to train your dog. Dogs are only going to be harder to train as each day goes by. At a certain point, getting him to learn one new command is nigh impossible.

Let me help you learn how you can train your dog right at home in amazing ways that both you and your dog will enjoy and love. It does not take that much time and effort. So, don't delay and start training your dog today!

Chapter 1: Why Positive Reinforcement Training is Perfect for Your Dog

Before we begin, let us discuss some popular training methods out there. That way, you understand exactly how positive reinforcement training is ideal for your dog. I will be honest; I had a good discussion with my fellow dog trainers both at work and online about which training method is both effective and ethical. Some training methods borrow certain elements from others.

Scientific Training

Scientific dog training is hard to define. However, it is used as a base for all other types of training because all methods are based on science. Science-based training relies on information that is continually being improved. It uses what we know about dogs such as their nature, their ability to be conditioned, and effectiveness of punishment and rewards, both of which are core to any training. Animal behaviorists are discovering new things about the psychology of dogs, so the information will keep changing. That also means that the training methods will also evolve. We may not be able to fully understand our canine friends, but at least we can rest assured that every new bit of information is an improvement to what we already know.

Since science-based dog training is so broad, it is hard to specify the exact methodology behind it. In reality, many of the methods used in scientific dog training are used in other forms of dog training as well. One of which is operant conditioning that covers positive reinforcement and certain forms of punishment. It is also worth pointing out that, in positive reinforcement training and other training methods I will show you, a reward is needed to successfully train your dog. However, it does not mean that you need to rely on treats. They are necessary at the start of the training, but you can phase them out with pats or praise.

Scientific training is the building block of all other training types. However, it is not for ordinary people as it is tedious to keep up with all the updates on studies. Therefore, it is best to leave it to professional trainers to take this information and turn it into a viable training method. Nonetheless, it is worth to stay somewhat informed about new research.

Dominance Training

You see, dogs are pack animals. They travel in groups, and there is always a leader called the alpha dog. Dogs see you as part of their pack. Using this instinctual pack mentality, we can create a training method that uses a relationship of appropriate submission and dominance. This is the whole idea of dominance-based training. We use the dog's pack hierarchy to get them to behave a certain way. The theory suggests that when dogs see themselves as the alpha, they misbehave. Therefore, you need to teach them that you are the alpha of the pack, and they need to submit.

This technique requires you to understand your dog's body language and respond appropriately so that you project confidence and authority. In the end, your dog will be obedient. He will be right behind you when you take him out for walks. You are the one who walks through the door first. If your dog wants to go out, he will sit and wait patiently before you open the door. If he wants to eat, he needs to wait for you while you prepare food.

As you may have already guessed, this kind of training requires strict rules. That means no dog on the furniture such as the couch, let alone the bed. You must not get down to your dog's eye level as well. These things make your dog believe that he is equal to, if not higher than you in the pack hierarchy. In this training method, you need to show your dog that you are in charge. You are the alpha in the house.

Currently, dominance training is believed to be outdated, as studies show that the pack dynamic of wolves in the wild is not the same for dogs. Plus, while dominance training can help curb undesirable behavior, it does not address the underlying problem. This can lead your dog to feel anxious or fearful, which is not healthy for him at all. Moreover, you need to maintain dominance over your dog, which can be difficult and dangerous for children and the elderly.

Mirror Training

Also known as model-rival training, it relies on the fact that dogs learn by observation. When you provide a model of good behavior or a rival to compete for resources, they learn to mimic the behavior. Your dog, as an observer, learns what he should do from the model. The model can also be about a rival who competes to perform the right task to get a desired toy or treat as a reward. It can either be a treat or toy, so long as it interests your dog so that he is encouraged to pick up the task and accomplish it quicker than his rival.

In this training, you (trainer) are the model, and you offer him rewards whenever he mimics good behavior. This training works because it uses dogs' natural instincts to socialize. In other words, your dog learns by example.

Mirror training is just as successful as operant conditioning and positive reinforcement. Certain trainers prefer mirror training over other positive reinforcement training methods because they feel mirror training is more natural and preferable. If your dog has a strong bond with you, both you and he can invest a lot of time to allow him to observe you and learn from you.

Relationship-Based Training

Relationship-based training utilizes many different training methods, but it adds a personal flair that is suitable for both the dog and his owner. It relies on the relationship between the dog and the trainer by meeting their needs through communication and by strengthening the bond. In short, the training is mutually beneficial.

This training method requires you to understand your dog's body language, what reward motivates him most, and how to meet his basic needs before each training session. Positive reinforcement certainly encourages good behavior through reward, but you also need to consider the environment in which the dog is trained. Control the environment to limit possible unwanted behavior.

For instance, suppose you want to teach your dog the "Sit" command. You need to teach him in a quiet place in your home first and practice until he is proficient with the command. You can thengradually have him practice in a noisier environment. When your dog fails to perform a command, you need to figure out why, instead of just punishing him. Remember that distraction, inability to hear, and unwillingness to perform are some of the most common reasons.

Relationship-based training creates a deep and meaningful bond, but it takes a lot of time and patience. Relationship-based training is not that much different from other methods if you do not count the personalized approach.

Electronic Training

Electronic training is among the cruelest training methods out there. It relies on the use of an electric collar to either shock or spray the dog with citronella upon activation. It is mainly used to train dogs at a distance when a leash is not applicable. For instance, shock collars can train a dog to stay in a certain boundary of an unfenced yard. I have seen it being used on dogs to work in fields or do hunting work. Shock collars are obviously safer than choke collars or other mechanical devices, but that does not mean you should use them.

There are plenty of issues with this training method. For one, it is the opposite of positive reinforcement. It relies on punishment for bad behavior. This teaches your dog what not to do, but does not tell him what he should do. You may already see the flaws here. In any given task, there is one correct choice or action. Your dog may have to suffer through trials and errors just to find that one right thing to do. It is very stressful for your dog and can lead to permanent anxiety issues.

I will not deny the fact that electric collar training can get results quickly, but it is only effective in the hands of professionals. Certified dog trainers only use electric collars when other options have been exhausted. Unfortunately, many inexperienced dog owners turn to this methodsimply because it gets results quickly. They tend to overuse the collars, therefore, subjecting their dogs to unnecessary stress and pain. There are many other alternatives out there that are far less stressful and painful. If you really consider using electric collars, make sure you consult a professional about the proper use. If worse comes to worst, I suggest you let a professional handle the training of your dog from here, so he does not have to be put under unnecessary stress and pain.

Clicker Training

Clicker training also utilizes operant conditioning that I mentioned earlier. It uses the principle of positive reinforcement, which we will discuss in a moment. In fact, clicker training is under the positive reinforcement umbrella. Clicker training simply uses a device that makes a quick, sharp, and distinct noise such as a whistle or a click to signal the dog when he has accomplished a wanted behavior.

The upside of clicker training is that it tells your dog exactly when he has got something right and knows he is going to get rewarded. The click itself is associated with the reward. You can use the clicker to easily teach your dog new behavior in addition to adding verbal commands.

The practice is simple. First, your dog needs to be conditioned to know that a click means that he is being rewarded. Then, you can train your dog, so he knows how to associate a certain behavior to the click and the reward. Finally, you can add verbal commandsto introduce a new form of association.

This type of training is very effective when you try to teach your dog new tricks. It is, however, not much so when you need to curb unwanted behavior. You can even use it to train your dog to perform complicated tasks. Many professional trainers also use clicker training. When you combine this training method with others, it can be an effective way to train your dog.

A word of warning, though. Some people have reported issues with this training method. While it is one of the easiest methods of dog training in the short term, it may be counterproductive in the long run. The problem is that your dog may become conditioned to the click and will not obey commands without it. Moreover, you need to have excellent timing skills. A split second delay in your click can result in the wrong action being registered, which may confuse your dog. Therefore, I advise you to phase away from the click and treat as a reward as soon as possible to prevent your dog from developing a dependency on the click.

Positive Reinforcement

We will focus on positive reinforcement in this book because I believe this is the best training method. This training method is popularized by trainers such as Dawn Sylvia-Stasiewicz who trained Bo, Obama's dog.

Dogs will repeat good behavior when you give them rewards. Punishment is the lack of reward, nothing more. So, if your dog is being naughty, he gets nothing. That way, he knows when he has done something right and when he has done something wrong. You can step up the punishment further by taking his treats or toys away. Since this does not involve physical punishment, your dog will not become permanently anxious or hurt emotionally or physically.

Just like clicker training, this training method starts by rewarding your dog when he has accomplished the desired behavior, immediately (or within seconds) after it happens. That way, your dog associates that behavior with the reward, so he is encouraged to repeat such behavior again for the reward. Some professional trainers use this alongside clicker training. This kind of training tells your dog exactly when he has completed the desired behavior. You can improve its effectiveness by using short commands such as sit, stay, and come.

Positive reinforcement requires consistency. That means that everyone in your home needs to use the same commands and follow the same reward system for this kind of training to be effective. First, start by rewarding your dog continuously whenever he does the right thing. Then, you can begin to give rewards less frequently as you observe that the behavior has become a habit. That is when your dog no longer performs a certain behavior just to get rewards.

Beginner trainers may accidentally reward bad behavior, such as letting the dog out when he barks at a squirrel or another dog. Simply correct this erroneous behavior by withholding rewards, and it should change eventually. As you can tell, it will take some time. Certain negative behavior is hard to curb when rewarding as-is, so you need to punish your dog by not giving him reward as well,so that he candevelop an alternative desired behavior.

Rewards do not have to be treated alone. You can also use toys, praises, or pets, and you should because it is easy to overfeed your dog when he is learning. I suggest you use small treats in the early stage, and then move to toys, praises, then pats as rewards as the behavior becomes more natural. You can even move to reward your dog intermittently as well, although I suggest you pet him as often as you can if he is being a good boy.

Again, this kind of training is best used to teach dogs new behavior, but is not so effective if you try to curb unwanted behavior. All it takes is patience, though.

In reality, there is no one-size-fits-all here. Each training method is most effective in a certain scenario. Out of all the training methods I have described above, the best one for your circumstance is positive reinforcement. It is quick, effective, and so simple that even first-time dog owners can teach their dogs to behave properly without hurting their pets. Your mileage may vary, though, as dogs may respond differently under the same training method. Even so, positive reinforcement is the way to go for common dog-owners.

Chapter 2: Prep Works

Before you even begin to train your dog, there are a few things you should know, so that the training process goes smoothly.

Choosing the Right Dog

First, keep in mind that a dog is one of the most rewarding pets, but also one of the most demanding. You cannot just get one, give him food, water, some toys, and be done with him. Dogs require more maintenance than a goldfish. I have personally met quite a few dog owners who want to give their dogs up to the animal shelter simply because they behave poorly or because they want a cute puppy, not a big old dog.

So, before you adopt (I highly recommend you adopt rather than buy) or buy a dog, consider whether it is time to have a dog in your life and your home and whether you can commit to taking care of your pet for at least 15 years, if not more. If yes, consider the following:

1. Does everyone in your home want a dog? You want to set out each person's responsibility right from the start to avoid confusing your dog. Also, think of the ground rules ahead of time.
2. Can you afford the time to provide exercises such as walks and play, in all kinds of weather or at night, and give him enough daily attention?
3. Do you have time to give him the training and socialization he needs throughout his life? Depending on where you live, you may be legally responsible for your dog's behavior to make sure that training and socialization are done correctly.
4. Can you afford bills such as annual vaccinations and regular de-worming? There are also other expenses to consider likehow to maintain your dog's diet, so he remains in good condition. If you travel often and do not want to take your dog with you, can you afford boarding kennel costs?
5. Most importantly, can you provide your dog with a safe and secure home for the rest of his life?

Keep in mind that you are responsible for your dog's behavior, both good or bad. Therefore, your dog must be taught good manners and be well-socialized. If certain misfortune occurs and you cannot care for your dog any longer, a dog with bad manners may face an uncertain future.

Which Dog to Choose

As of now, there are so many breeds to choose from. The rule of thumb is to stick with the breeds that suit you best. For instance, a terrier will have a different temperament from a herding breed. A guarding breed will behave differently from a toy breed. There are plenty of books and magazines out there that you can get all the information you need on breed differences. You are not in a hurry at this point, so take as long as you need to thoroughly conduct your research before you commit. There are also breed rescue societies that are dedicated to certain breeds, and other websites you can find that provide good, bite-sized information on dogs. A good place to start is https://uk.pedigree.com/getting-a-dog/breed-selector.

If you are more into crossbred dogs, keep in mind that it is a lot harder to determine their characteristics as we do not know beforehand what the predominant behavior trait could be. In that case, you can narrow down your expectations by getting as much information from the individual dog as you can. Still, many crossbred dogs generally have the best traits of both parents and are still good boys.

Taking on an Adult Dog

An adult dog is probably a better idea for you if you do not want to go through all of the intensive training you need to provide for your pup. However, know that dogs learn things a lot faster when they are young, so you will miss out on the golden opportunity to train your dog effectively. That does not mean that older dogs cannot learn anything new. It just takes more time, especially if your training methods are different from the previous dog owner.

On the plus side, dogs are probably housetrained and more settled than puppies. Separation anxiety should already be addressed too. Your dog should have passed the chewing and destructive stage of life, and certain habits may have already been formed, good or bad.

All in all, it is a dice roll. But if you got your dog from a reputable shelter or dog breeder, you should not have any problems with him. At the very least, you know what the dog is like from the start, so you know what you are getting yourself into. If you decide to get an adult dog, chances are that he will either be from a charity such as Blue Cross, a private home that cannot look after the dog, or a breed rescue club.

If you decide to adopt one from a charity center, make sure to talk to the staff. They know all about the animals under their care intimately and know which dog suits you best. The goal of any rescue shelter is to find a long-term and loving home for dogs that were victims of circumstances. Dogs from such shelters generally have negative behaviors tied to their traumatic experience. For instance, abused dogs may yelp uncontrollably, if you approach them suddenly or even bite your hand if you reach out to pat them too quickly. These dogs have a bad start in life, and most of the time, it is not their fault. Whatever negative behavior they have, the staff will let you know, and you can decide. By the time you visit them, the dogs should have mostly recovered from their unfortunate past. Still, keep in mind that there are negative behaviors you should watch out for.

When choosing a dog, do not pick one based on their looks. You need to know the dog's temperament and previous history. For instance, a rescue dog may despise cats, or may not be able to live with children. If the dog has behavioral problems such that it cannot be left alone for long periods of time, the staff is more than willing to give you advice and provide assistance to help you overcome the problem. I always adopt dogs from a shelter that has dogs that had a traumatic experience in the past. It is a bold move, even for me because taking care of these dogs can be very difficult. However, I am a firm believer that dogs like these deserve better. The struggle to raise one is real, but the love you get back in returnfor turning the poor mug's life around is more than enough to make up for it.

For pure breeds, the breed rescue club should be able to give you advice about the characteristics of the specific breed you want, as well as about any other dogs they are trying to find a home for.

Choosing Your Dog

Now that you have done your research and have spoken to the staff or previous owner, it is time to answer yet another set of questions. I know. It's rather tedious, but trust me. You would rather get the right dog later than the wrong dog sooner.

1. Have you obtained enough information about the dog's history and preferences?
2. Have you had a chance to go for a "test run" by taking a walk or playing together to see what the dog may be like away from the kennels, or away from home?
3. Do you have a full veterinary history? What operations or illnesses has the dog had? What vaccinations has he gotten and have you seen the proof such as the vaccination certificate? Other than that, make sure you have a written agreement that taking the dog is subject to a satisfactory veterinary inspection within 72 hours of your doing so.
4. What help or advice do you have access to if there are veterinary or behavioral problems after you have adopted the dog?

If your dog is a rescue dog, try to gather as much information as you can. If you are rehoming a dog from a charity or breed rescue club, make sure there is a pet insurance cover that covers any early, unforeseen veterinary costs.

Other Things to Consider

- Veterinary treatment can be costly, so I recommend you get pet insurance. There are many different policies out there, so make sure to speak to your veterinary practice.
- Depending on where you live, you may be legally obligated to have a dog collar and tag detailing your dog's name and address whenever he is out in public. Moreover, all dogs above the age of eight weeks must be micro-chipped, again in certain countries. A microchip is a harmless computer chip the size of a grain of rice that contains a unique code that matches up to your pet's details. Think of an ID card... for your dog. Such a chip is usually placed inside the dog's neck and will be scanned using a scanner to

collect the data. Puppies should be chipped before leaving the breeder or rescue center. So, make sure you do your research about your country's laws before adopting a dog.

- If you are traveling and cannot take your dog with you, it is a good idea to take him to a boarding kennel. You can book a place for your dog to stay for a long time in advance. They need to see an up-to-date vaccination record, though.

- Exercise is crucial to your dog's health. How much exercise a dog needs depends on the breed of your dog, but a good walk every day is the bare minimum.

- Training is an ongoing process. You can teach an old dog new tricks, albeit it will take longer. In any case, it is worth training your dog, so find training classes locally. Vets' practices, rescue centers, and dog wardens should have details about classes your dog could attend.

If you have done your research carefully and made sure that you are fully prepared and able to dedicate the time, money, and energy on your dog, you will be handsomely rewarded. If you run into problems or need advice, organizations like Blue Cross or the Association of Pet Behavior Counsellors should be able to help you.

Welcoming Your Dog

Now that you have all the information you need and have decided which dog you want to adopt, it is time to do some work at your own home to make sure the transition from the shelter to your place is comfortable for your dog.

Before Bringing Your Dog Home

- Stock up: You need all sorts of supplies for your dog. Make sure to have a leash, collar, ID tag, crate (or gate as needed), bed, bowls, food, treats, toys, grooming supplies, waste bags, and enzymatic cleaner.

- Dog-proof your home: Find and remove hazardous items and valuable items that your dog could chew or swallow.

- Set up your house: Make sure you know where the dog's crate, bed, and bowls will go. Think of where the food, treats, and supplies will be stored. Make sure everyone knows where everything is.

- Decide on the dog's schedule (more on that later) for walks, play, feeding, training, and potty time, and who is responsible for each activity.

The First Day:

- Means of travel: Think ahead of the time where the dog will ride on the way home. It is best to have two people collect the dog. One to drive and the other to pay attention to him. Have some towels handy just in case your dog becomes sick on the way home.

- Bring the dog straight home: Make his travel direct and brief. Do not run errands along the way. You want your dog home as soon as possible.

- No parties: Some people I have worked with throw parties for dogs that just arrived home. This is not ideal because the dog may become overexcited and overwhelmed. Limit or discourage visitors for the first few days, so that your dog has time to adjust to his new home in peace. If possible, make his arrival as quiet and low-key as possible.

- Let your dog explore: Dogs are curious creatures, and they will explore their surrounding the moment they arrive. So, let your pooch familiarize himself with his surroundings. Let him sniff around the yard or outdoor area near your home, on a leash of course.

- Introduce your dog: Let your dog get to know your family members outside, one at a time. Keep everything calm and low-key. Do not approach the dog yourself. Let the dog take the initiative to approach, sniff, and lead the interaction. Giving your dog treats helps him associate everyone in the house with pleasant things. During the initial introduction, refrain from hugging, kissing, picking up, staring at, or patting the top of his head. These things can be frightening for your dog at first. Don't worry; you can do that later when your dog is more accustomed to everyone.

- Stay close to home: Do not take your dog on long excursions outside. Stick close to home for now. You want to learn your new dog's behavior before you can reliably determine how he responds to different stimulus. Try to create a controlled environment in which your dog roams. Create a walking routine in an area that is quiet but familiar. A structured play also provides a means to exercise, bond, and train.

- Give your dog a tour: When your dog goes exploring, make sure to have a leash on him just in case he does something naughty. Try to keep the mood calm and relaxed. Dissuade him from chewing or grabbing any objects with a "leave it" command. If he has not learned this command beforehand, then simply offer him a new toy.

- Take your dog outside often: Dogs do not generalize as well as we do. Even if your dog has been housetrained previously, he needs to learn your new house rules. This includes a housetraining refresher course, although it will not take as long for him to relearn this. If your dog is housetrained, it is worth asking the previous owner how the dog was trained so that you can follow the same training methods and effectively train your dog.

- Make sure your dog gets enough "quiet time": That way, he can acclimate to the new surroundings. Observe how your dog behaves during this time.

- If you have a resident dog(s), have the first meeting outside: One at a time if you have more than one. Do not rush the introduction. Keep the leashes loose on all dogs without tension. They should meet in a food-free and toy-free zone. As they mingle, observe, and manage their interactions. Do not leave them alone together until you are absolutely sure that it is safe. When you take your dogs out for a walk, have a different person walk each dog.

- If you have a resident cat(s), keep the cat safe: Puppies should have no problem interacting with cats. Dogs, on the other hand, can cause problems. Unless you know how the dog will react, the interaction may go poorly if you do not control it. Use doors, gates, and leashes to prevent contact at first. Do not give your dog the opportunity to chase the cat because if he does, he will go for it and both the cat and dog will not spare your furniture as they run around. By then, it will be too late to do anything. Other than that, make sure your cat has escape options. Keep encounters brief and manage all interactions.

Create Daily Routines:

- Sleeping: At first, the crate or dog bed should be close to where you sleep just in case your dog experiences separation anxiety. It should already be addressed by the previous owner, but it's worth helping him ease into his new home by doing this again. In the end, you want his bed or crate to be in a room that is safe, dog-proofed, easily cleaned, cozy, quiet, and with familiar scents. Do not put your dog in an inhibited area such as the garage or basement.

- Feeding: Check with your vet about what food you should feed your dog and how much based on their breed, size, age, activity level, and health. If possible, it is better to feed your dog two smaller meals a day rather than one large meal. The reason is that you need to make room by reducing meal size to allow for treats during training. Treats will not be effective as a training reward if your dog is on a full stomach. Also, make sure that the food bowl is in a safe area – as far away from foot traffic as possible.

- Walks: Initially, walks should only be 5 to 10 minutes long until you know your dog's new behavior and how he responds to different stimuli. Again, take your dog to quiet places at first and avoid interactions with other dogs and unfamiliar people until both you and your dog are comfortable with one another.

- Chew/interactive toys: Crates and other appropriate toys are great ways to keep your dog busy and out of trouble. How you manage your dog's behavior and environment prevents problematic behaviors. For instance, chew toys are a great way to direct your dog's attention to appropriate toys, and away from objects that you do not want your dog to chew on e.g. your new and expensive pair of sneakers. Interactive toys stimulate your dog's mind. You can physically tire your dog by taking him out for walks or by playing games with him, but he also needs mental stimulus. Dogs tend to chew or dig when they are bored, so interactive toys are designed to address that problem. With a new dog, avoid rough and tumble, slapping, wrestling, and chasing games because he does not know you well and may think that you are threatening him, not playing with him.

How to Schedule Your Dog's Daily Life

Dogs are creatures of habit. We don't want to lead a routine life as it is boring. Dogs, however, need one to follow. They can decide on their own what they want to do throughout the day, but it is better if you decide for them. Left to their own devices, dogs may pick up undesirable behaviors that are very tricky to curb. Then again, the same can be said for us.

Schedules are very crucial for your dog. You need to have a precise feeding, exercise, and potty time. Creating a schedule should also involve everyone in the house so that everyone is involved in caring for the dog, not to mention making every day consistent for him, which is something you should always strive for.

Other than being a creature of habit, a precise schedule makes your dog happy. He knows what to expect at a certain time during the day, which gives him a sense of security. It has practical values because it keeps everyone in the house on the same page as far as who is responsible for each task. Scheduling your dog's daily activities also makes it easier for you to train and control your dog. Housetraining is much more efficient if you have a schedule.

Scheduling Food

Make sure that everyone in the house feeds your dog precisely in terms of the amount of food, feeding time, the way of feeding, and where the dog eats. The package of the dog food should have instructions on how to feed your dog. Make sure you follow those instructions and that there is enough water for your dog. Other than that, I recommend you take your dog out so he can do his business outside right after mealtime.

If you know exactly when your dog eats and drinks, you should have a good idea when he needs to go outside to take care of his business. You also get to train his digestive system to adapt to the schedule, which is extremely helpful when you are housetraining him.

Potty Scheduling

As I have mentioned earlier, when it comes to potty, it is best to think ahead. Take your dog outside at the first sign that he needs to go to the bathroom. This is when your dog starts to scratch at the door or whine as he circles it. If you wait until he squats down, it is already too late. So, do not wait and run the risk of him accidentally soiling the inside of your house.

If you are precise about his feeding and drinking time, then your dog should also have a predictable time when he needs to hit the bathroom. The more you get him to do it outside, the less likely it will be for him to have an accident indoors. In the early phase of his potty training, make sure to keep an eye on him in case he wanders off and causes an accident in the house. You want to be able to respond immediately at the first sign that he needs to hit the bathroom. If an accident occurs in the house, just make sure to dispose of the waste and clean the area thoroughly with an odor neutralizing cleaner, so that your dog does not cause an accident in the same place again.

As always, never scold or punish your dog after an accident. It will only serve to ruin the relationship you have built so far. If your dog wants to go inside the house, clap loudly or say, "No." Then, quickly take him outside and reward him then and there. The fact is that dogs want to make you happy and you just need to tell them how. The clearer you show him that he has his own bathroom outside, the quicker he catches on to the idea.

Scheduling Exercise and Play

Exercise is one of the most important things for a dog in terms of health. It is beneficial for both of you as well because your dog won't use the extra energy to pursue destructive behaviors. Without exercise, your dog can exhibit excessive chewing or other destructive behaviors,once he becomes bored or tries to burn off the extra energy. A tired dog (through training and playing!) is a happy dog. If you continue to neglect him, your dog may become overweight due to the simple fact that he does not have the opportunity to burn off the calories he picks up during mealtime. So, take some time to walk your dog to get in some exercise for both of you. Moreover, he can use this opportunity to socialize with other humans and animals. This also presents an opportunity for you to strengthen your bond with your dog while doing something together.

Chapter 3: Key Principles to Training an Amazing Dog

In this chapter, I will cover what we will discuss in the upcoming chapters. Consider this to be the basic principles to help you understand why it is a good idea to train your dog a certain way. All of these are going to be useful in potty training, house training, clicker training, dealing with problematic behaviors, etc. What you will find here are all the essentials to training your dog.

Why Positive Reinforcement?

Reinforcement means making a certain behavior more likely. In this case, we want to focus on positive behavior. The idea here is to give your dog a good reason to repeat good behavior. There is nothing better than the promise of rewards for your dog. With treats, toys, affection, and praise, your dog is convinced that making you happy is in his best interest.

Training with reward is all about teaching your dog that if he makes good choices, he will be rewarded generously. When your dog is rewarded, he will associate the reward with his behavior and will be more likely to do it again in the future. For instance, if your dog gets a treat whenever he sits when you tell him to, he will be more likely to do this again the next time you say sit.

Positive reinforcement is the best way to encourage your dog to behave a certain way on a daily basis. For one, science tells us that reward-based training is much more effective than punishment-based training. Plus, positive reinforcement is exciting for both you and your dog, and it helps build trust and a positive bond between you and your dog. Moreover, many dog owners that use reward-based training report fewer behavioral problems in their dogs. Finally, reward-based training builds confidence in your dogs and teaches them to think for themselves.

How Positive Reinforcement Is Applied

I will explain in more details about each training such as potty and house training, but all of them follow certain patterns:

Make It Worthwhile

As I have mentioned earlier, the key to positive reinforcement is to convince your dog that it is worth his effort to do what you want. When it comes to rewards, there are so many things you can give him, but there are only a few that are worthy enough to compel him to behave a certain way. The reward should be something that your dog loves, such as treats, toys, or going out for walks. There is no one-size-fits-all here, so you need to experiment to see what your dog loves the most. Use this to reward your pooch. It is worth making a list of what your dog loves, from most favorite to least favorite. I'll tell you why in a second.

Reward Good Behavior

Whenever your dog behaves in a way that you are satisfied with, make sure to let him know by rewarding him. Again, use a reward that your dog really loves. When it comes to passive behaviors such as being quiet or calm, reward your dog with pats or praise with a calm voice so as not to make him excited. If he does something active such as running to you when you call him, then reflect his energy and reward him.

Think About Phasing Out Rewards

Some dog owners I know are guilty of overfeeding their dogs because they rely on treats as rewards. You don't want to overfeed your dog, nor do you want him to shrug you off because what you give him is not rewarding. While you need to reward your dog every time he is successful in displaying a behavior, consider falling back to something that is healthy but still rewarding. Remember the list I advised you to make? If the top favorite thing is treats, then consider falling back on toys, walks, or praise. If your dog enjoys pats or praisesmore than treats or toys, then this is great news!

When dogs learn new behaviors, you need to make sure that they can perform it in a different environment. Then, you can change up the reward, so that you do not give your dog treats for the rest of his life. Also, consider rewarding intermittently. When your dog is so used to the behavior that he starts doing it instinctively, you do not have to reward him as often anymore.

For example, at the start of the training stage, you can use treats to reward your dog as it is one of the best rewards out there. Whenever he does something successfully, give him treats. When your dog becomes proficient with a command or behavior, start alternating the reward like replacing the treats with praise or pats instead. From there, always pat or praise your dog and give him a treat once every three to five times when he successfully executes the behavior. You can even mix up the rewards, so your dog does not know when he will get the treat. This keeps him interested.

Get The Timing Right

Dogs live in the moment. They will forget what they did a few minutes ago, so you need to make sure you reward your dog as soon as he does what you told him. It is useful to have something to mark the exact moment when your dog did what they were supposed to do. This is why clicker training is effective as it allows you to produce a loud and distinct click, so your dog knows the exact moment he did something right. The click tells your dog that he did something you are happy about, and a reward is coming his way. Of course, praises work just as well. Having the clicker is handy, but not necessary. Some people have reported that using the clicker creates a dependency on the click. Take this into consideration as well if you want to use clicker training.

Whatever it is, make sure you choose a marker and stick to it, so your dog does not get confused. When you are training your dog, make sure to signal the exact moment when he is doing something you want him to do. That way, he knows what he should do to get the reward.

Positive Reinforcement as a Way of Life

As long as you keep in mind that any behavior that your dog finds rewarding is something he is likely to do again, you can set things up in a way that you reward him for doing good. This involves planning ahead so you can reward your dog with something they like whenever you see them behaving the way you want. Eventually, good behavior will become a habit for your dog. He will repeat it to the point that he cannot misbehave.

Different Rewards for Different Times and Places

There may be times when your dog needs an extra or different reward. In such cases, he may feel safe and comfortable in your home, but pulling off the exact same command in a crowded environment is nigh impossible for him as there are so many distractions. So, some of the things that excite him at home may be ineffective outside. If your dog cannot respond to you because of distractions, you should change up the reward system to keep him interested. For instance, he may be content with sitting in one place for a piece of treat at home, but when he is out with you, the treat may not be enticing enough. Therefore, consider using something juicier such as his favorite treat, a larger snack, a game, or a toy. Again, consult the list. It is probably a good idea to try using the third best reward for in-home training and alternate that with second best, and then using the best reward for special occasions such as this one.

If Your Dog Behaves Poorly

If your dog behaves badly and consistently, do not punish him by hitting or yelling at him. Instead, think of the underlying reason. Perhaps your dog is bored. Maybe he is anxious. Your dog may be suffering from separation anxiety. We will discuss addressing problematic behaviors in Chapter 9. From what we have learned from positive reinforcement, whatever the dog finds enjoyable is something he will do more frequently. In this case, if he keeps behaving badly for a long time, perhaps the underlying problem is the fact that the behavior itself is rewarding. For instance, if your dog loves to jump and cling to you whenever you get home, your first response may be to tell him to get down and try to hold him down, so he does not mess your clothes. If your dog enjoys the attention and physical contact, the action of you pushing him down and telling him to get down are rewarding for him. So, he may do it again next time even though you thought that you did not give him any reward for his behavior.

In such a situation, think about how you can guide your dog to behave better. One solution is to not give him anything, even attention. The lack of reward is punishing enough. If your dog loves jumping and clinging to you, just turn your back to him and do not give him any attention until he calms down. You can then reward him with attention. This tells your dog that being hyper-energetic whenever he sees you is not going to get him anything. He will eventually learn that if he remains quiet and calm, he will get the attention he wants.

In some cases, your dog may have a bad habit of digging up your yard. In this case, your ignoring him is not going to work either. You need to dissuade him from bad behavior and then provide a better alternative and generously reward him for choosing the desired alternative.

The desired alternative is another kind of behavior that you want your dog to display. The key here is to know exactly why your dog behaves that way. Using our jumping and clinging dog example, perhaps your dog is just excited about meeting people. In that case, you can use it as a reward for him. For instance, you can ask him to sit and reward him before he gets up to see someone.

Other Training Tips

Here are some other tips you should consider when you want to train your dog:

Choose Your Dog's Name Wisely

You want to pick a name for your dog that reflects his personality and is something that you love. It is worth considering the practical side of things as well when you try to come up with a name. You want to have a name that is short and has a strong consonant. That way, your dog can hear you calling his name clearly. Consider Jasper, Jack, Ginger, etc. If it's an old dog, he is probably used to his name. That does not mean you cannot change it, though.

If you adopted him from the shelter, he should have a temporary name given to him by the staff. It's worth asking them what name he goes by, and perhaps you can stick with it if it is viable. If you got your dog from a breeder, he probably has a long name. Try to be creative and shorten it. If your dog had been through an abusive situation, it is a good idea to give him a new name to represent a clean slate. Having a new name is a fresh start for your dog, which allows him to overcome his trauma.

Thankfully, dogs can adapt very easily. With consistency and time, your dog will respond to his new name. Whatever his name is, make sure to associate it with pleasant and fun things rather than negative. The idea is for him to think of his name the same way he thinks of other fun things in his life, such as "food," "good boy," or "walk."

Think of the House Rules

Before your dog comes home, think of what he can and cannot do. Is he allowed on the couch or bed? What part of the house is off limits? Does he have his own chair at the dinner table or will he eat from a bowl on the floor? These things are often neglected by new dog owners. Most of the time, people just tell their dogs what not to do only when whatever it is their dog does get annoying. Doing so can confuse your dog, so be clear about the rules right off the bat.

Set Up Your Dog's Private Den

Your dog needs privacy just like you. He needs a room of his own. So, introduce him to his new room, as soon as possible. Consider a place that is not used by anyone else in the family or another pet. Having some quiet time alone can help calm your dog, whereas he would feel anxious or exposed if he were to sleep elsewhere. Of course, it will take some time for him to get used to sleeping away from you, especially if he is a young dog. For his private space, consider using a crate as it is an invaluable tool for housetraining and it also functions as his den.

Help Your Dog Relax

Especially for a dog that has had a nasty experience with an abusive owner, making sure that your home is a safe place is crucial. So, as soon as your dog gets home, give him a warm hot water bottle and a ticking clock near his sleeping area. At the start, I recommend having your dog sleep close to you, preferably right next to your bed, so he can start to trust and get accustomed to your presence. The hot water bottle and ticking clock are needed to comfort him as they imitate the heat and heartbeat of his littermates. This is even more important if you got your dog from a busy and loud shelter as he is so used to the crowd that the quiet environment of your home is almost haunting. Do not rush your dog, though. Let him take his time exploring your home and have him sleep close to you for the first few nights. Do whatever you can to help him get comfortable with his new home, which will be beneficial for both you and your dog.

Teach Him to Come when Called

First and foremost, make sure your dog knows his name and that he should come to you when you say it. This is one of the most important commands your dog should master. When it comes to commands, we tend to lean a little bit on dominance training as one side is the one giving orders and the other just obeys. But we will not be using dominance training elements here. So, when your dog comes to you, get to his level (be on the same eye-level with him) and reward him generously. We want to use positive reinforcement to our advantage when training our dogs. From there, try to call him when he is busy doing something interesting. Getting this command down is very useful as you can stop him from doing something dangerous.

Reward Good Behavior

This is the entire idea of positive reinforcement. Rewards can be toys, treats, pats, or praise. The first two are needed in the training process, but you need to shift to the latter two as your dog becomes more proficient with the command. On that note, do not reward bad behavior as it will only confuse him. Ignoring him whenever he does something bad is already a punishment when attention is a reward.

Curb the Jumping

Dogs love to jump and cling to you as a form of greeting. To be fair, that is super adorable, but not everyone appreciates this behavior. Do not reprimand your dog whenever he does this. Instead, just ignore him until he settles down. Then, reward him for his calming down with pats or praise. Do not encourage your dog's jumping behavior by reflecting his level of energy and excitement as this also rewards him. Instead, just turn your back to him and pay him no mind until he calms down.

"Dog Time"

Dogs live in the moment. They do not have the ability to plan ahead. They forget something they did only a few minutes ago. This is why you need to take every opportunity you get to train your dog to behave the right way. There is no point in trying to tell him what he did wrong an hour ago. When you see your dog doing something bad, take that opportunity to practice your training technique immediately, so your dog has a chance to correct his erroneous behavior. Through repetition, your dog will come to associate his wrongful behavior with the correction and choose the latter in the future. Plus, you reinforce what your dog has learned through repetition.

Curb the Biting and Nipping

Your dog should learn bite inhibition at a young age unless he was in a specific circumstance in which he did not get to mingle with other dogs. Bite inhibition is putting less force into the bite, which usually occurs during a play. Dogs learn this early on because if they bite too hard, other dogs ignore them. You can do the same if your dog loves to bite your pant leg or chew on your favorite shoe. Do not scold him. If he bites you, pretend that you are in great pain from the bite. Your dog should immediately stop as he will be so surprised that he unintentionally hurt you that much. Your dog does not want to hurt you, so he will stop biting when he learns that he is doing you harm. I find this trick to be very effective for younger dogs.

If this trick does not work, consider trading a chew toy for your pant leg or hand. This trick can be effective if your dog has taken a liking to your shoes. He should turn to chew on chew toys or bones because they are more interesting anyway. If this fails too, break up the biting behavior and ignore him. More on curbing bad behavior in Chapter 9.

Training Sessions

Training sessions should be short and interesting. As I have said earlier, dogs live in the moment and will forget the things they do in a few minutes. So, it is not worth dragging training on for long because, by the time you finish, your dog will have forgotten what the training was about. For example, instead of having a one 15-minute training session a day, consider training 3 times a day, 5 minutes each time. The latter is much more effective. Plus, you can incorporate games into the training sessions to make it fun for both you and your dog (more on that in Chapter 10).

Also, end the training session on a good note. He has worked hard to make you happy, so he deserves your praise and pats. You can take him out for walks, or set aside five minutes to play around with him. This ensures that your dog looks forward to the next class. He should show up with his tail wagging, ready for whatever you throw at him.

Patience

Dog training will take longer than puppy training, so be patient. Do not rush your dog or yell at him if he fails to pick up the command several times. If your training is not effective, there may be underlying problems. The environment may be full of distractions, so your dog cannot focus on you. In other cases, the command is too complex, or the behavior is not marked clearly. Try to find the underlying problem and address it before you proceed.

Consistency

Another thing worth noting is that your training must be consistent. For puppies, you can develop a certain training style and stick to it. You can do the same for your dogs, although it is more efficient if you follow the training style of the previous owner. If you wish to do the latter, ask the previous owner exactly how the dog was trained. Every single detail matters such as tone of voice, reward, etc. Be strictly consistent with your commands and training methods for the best result. For instance, if you teach your dog the "Sit" command, only say the word once and your dog should sit. In certain situations, the dog may become overexcited and the owner attempts to ground him by yelling "Sit! Sit! Sit!" It is not going to work because the dog only knows "Sit," not "Sit! Sit! Sit!" Your tone of voice and hand gesture should also be consistent.

Positive Reinforcement Rules

Positive reinforcement is a super effective tool to train your dog. However, it is not as simple as praising your dog for everything that he gets right. To maximize the effectiveness of positive reinforcement, you need to follow certain rules:

Do:

Immediately Praise and Reward Desired Behavior

Animals, especially dogs, live in the moment. They cannot think and plan ahead like us. Therefore, if you want your training to be effective, you need to provide an immediate response. This applies to both giving treats and affection. Reward whenever your dog does something you want him to do. For example, if you are potty training your dog, reward him every time he does his business at his designated location. Make sure to reward your dog every time he gets a command right.

Keep the Training Short and Fun

The idea is to get your dog to understand that good things come his way when he obeys you. As we said earlier though, dogs cannot tolerate boring training for long. So, try to make your training sessions short and fun. If possible, try to end the training on a good note by finishing it up with a successful command and a treat.

Phase Treats Out

While we are on the subject of treats, they are indeed necessary to entice your dog into listening to you. If you rely on treats too much, you run the risk of overfeeding your dog. It is okay to use them at the early phase of dog training, but you should wean your dog off of them because he may not obey your command without seeing the treat first. So, replace treats with affection and pats. Eventually, your dog should do what you want just to make you happy. In a way, your smile is rewarding enough. You can also associate a reward with certain sounds such as "Good Boy!" or a click from the clicker, which we will get to in a much later chapter. Eventually, you can take away the treat, and your dog should still respond to the sound.

Don't...

Make Things Complicated

Dogs can understand human speech through repetition. However, that does not mean you should come up with complicated commands as it will speed up the training process. If you want your dog to fetch his toy, don't use the command "Fetch, Mr. Goofy." It is long and overcomplicated. "Fetch" is much simpler with the addition of pointing to the toys. If your commands or training routine are too complicated, your dog will never be able to learn anything. Keep it short and simple.

Show Consistency

Along that line, make sure you are consistent if you want your dog to have a specific behavior. For instance, if you reward your dog for not jumping on the couch, you cannot let him come up there and give him pats. Doing so will only confuse your dog about what you really want. Moreover, and this is a common mistake, everyone else in the house also needs to follow the same rule. Your poor dog will be so confused if he has to remember what he needs to do for everyone. This also applies to commands. If you say "Sit" to get your dog to sit, others cannot use the command "Sit down" and expect your dog to sit.

Stop Correcting Your Dog

Another big mistake that I see dog owners make when it comes to positive reinforcement is that they cannot say no to their dogs. I understand that they are adorable, and I have made the same mistake in the past, but you need to correct wrongful behavior. Just make sure you keep the correction time separate from positive reinforcement time. Just like children, we need to teach our dogs discipline.

Chapter 4: Crate Training

Crate training is helpful if you have trained your dog properly. It gives your dog a sense of stability and safety when you want to put him in a cage. Plus, it also gives you a way to establish order and rule in your own home. If you crate train your dog properly, it is going to be beneficial for everyone, especially your dog.

The Crate Philosophy

Your dog should perceive the crate as its den. Dogs are naturally den animals. In the wild, the den is a safe space for your dog where he can rest, sleep, or fall back to without the fear of danger. For a domesticated dog, the crate serves as a safe haven. Initially, he will see it as confinement, which he despises. However, if you introduce and use it correctly, the crate is where your dog willingly chooses to sleep, hide, or simply hang around in because it's his own space.

Why Crate Training is Beneficial

There are many reasons why crate training your dog is a good idea.

House Training

The idea is that you want your dog to treat his crate like how a wild dog would his den. Your dog will not soil his own den, or his crate if he sees it as a den. Therefore, you can rest assured that your dog will take the first opportunity to relieve himself when you let him out. That, at least, allows you to define where he can do his business. Of course, crates aren't the only way to housetrain your dog, but crate training aligns with your dog's interest. Just make sure to take your dog out at regular intervals, so that he can go to the bathroom outside. That way, he learns where he needs to do his business.

Transporting

When you familiarize your dog with the crate early on, house training is only a stone throw away. Not only that, your dog will be comfortable with their future means of transportation. No longer will he bark, whine, or struggle inside the crate. This saves both you and your dog a lot of time and frustration. The crate is the best way to transport your dog, whether it is a short trip to the vet or a long road trip.

Teaching

Just like us, dogs need rules to know their place and boundaries. Crate training is the best way to start introducing your dogs to those limitations and creating a hierarchy in your house. Your dog will learn early on what he can and cannot do. When you put your dog in a crate when you are away or when you are busy, you restrict his access to the rest of the house so he cannot do any harm to your furniture, shoes, or rug. When you let your dog free, you will have to be attentive and reprimand him appropriately. As such, your dog learns right from the start that the crate is his very own space, and the rest of the house is your territory.

Choosing the Right Crate

As in anything in life, not all crates are created equal. There are many crates to choose from, and they are all best suited for different situations and dogs. The two best ones are plastic and metal crates.

Metal Crates

Metal crates are wire, metal crates that are ideal and a popular choice among dog owners. You see, they have a mesh-like, collapsible structure, which makes them very convenient. You can just disassemble and transport them with ease. Plus, metal crates provide a high level of ventilation and visibility. Similar to plastic crates, metal crates are very easy to clean in case your dog soils them by accident. They do not appear to be sturdy, but they do a perfect job of keeping dogs in, making them an ideal choice. You can be flexible with the space you want to give to your dog.

Plastic Crates

Plastic cratesare more for transportation purposes than for use as an in-house den for your dog. They provide less visibility and ventilation. However, they are great if you travel often and take your dog with you because all airlines require your dog to be placed in this crate to be transported. Plastic crates are also useful if your dog needs more security because they aremore secluded compared to metal dog crates. You can use plastic crates too if your home has a high level of activity because they give your dog more privacy.

A Note on Crate Size

No matter what crate you choose, you need to make sure that your dog has enough room in there. If he cannot stand up and turn around, then it is too small. On the other hand, do not buy one that is so large that your dog can just soil one corner and sleep in the other. This will make your house training efforts to go down the drain.

Personally, I suggest you get a metal crate in your home and a plastic crate for transportation. The metal crate is ideal in your home because you can customize its size with a movable divider. You need to buy new and larger plastic crates as your dog grows anyway.

Training Process

Depending on your dog's age, past experience, and temperament, it can take up to weeks to fully crate train your dog. You need to keep two things in mind. First, your dog should associate the crate with safety, privacy, and other pleasant emotions. Second, the training should not be rushed. It should be taken on a step-by-step basis.

Step 1: Introduce Your Dog to the Crate

First off, put the crate in your home where there is a lot of foot traffic and where many people hang around, such as the family room. Try to decorate the crate to make it look friendly. I recommend throwing a soft blanket or towel in there. Then, take off the door and let your dog explore the crate at his own leisure. Certain dogs will be curious and go in and sleep there right away. If that is not the case, do the following:

- Bring your dog to the crate and talk to him in a positive and happy tone of voice. Don't put your dog in the crate; just near it, so he is aware that the crate is there. Make sure the crate door is open and secured. You don't want the door to fall down and hit your dog as it will frighten him.

- Encourage your dog to enter the crate by dropping treats around the crate. Your dog should approach and eat the treats. Drop more just inside the door and then all the way inside. If your dog is still anxious and refuses to go all the way into the crate, that's fine. There is no need to force him to enter it.

- Rinse and repeat the previous step until your dog calmly enters the crate fully to get the food. If treats fail to get his attention, try putting his favorite toy in the crate. Remember, your dog may need several days before he is familiar with the crate.

Step 2: Feed Your Dog

When your dog is more familiar with the crate, the next step is to convince him that it is his private den. To do this, you need to feed him near the crate first to create a pleasant association with the crate:

- If your dog enters the crate calmly when you start this step, then place the food dish at the back of the crate.

- If your dog is still reluctant, note how far they are willing to go and place the food dish there. Do not force your pooch to go further inside because they will become fearful or anxious. Every time you feed them, put the dish a little further back, and work your way until your dog can eat at the deepest end of the crate.

- When your dog is finally comfortable eating in his crate, you can close the door while they are eating. For the first few days, open the door as soon as your dog is finished eating. From there, try leaving the door closed a few minutes longer. The goal is to make him patient enough to stay in the crate for about ten minutes after eating.

- If your dog starts to whine to be let out, then you may have increased the length of time too quickly. So, try to leave him for a shorter period next time. I also want to point out that you should not let your dog out immediately as he is whining. If you do that, he will learn that the way to get out of the crate is to whine, so he will keep doing it. Therefore, don't let your dog out unless he stops whining.

Step 3: Extend Crating Periods

After your dog is comfortable with eating inside their crate, the next step is to confine him in there for a short time while you are home.

- Start by calling your dog over to the crate and give him a treat.
- Give him a command to enter the crate. I personally use "kennel" as the command. Also, encourage your dog to enter by pointing to the inside of the crate while holding a treat in your hand.
- When your dog enters the crate, praise him, and give him a treat. Close the door.
- Sit quietly near the crate for ten minutes or so. Then, get up and go into another room for a few minutes. Repeat this one more time before letting your dog out of the crate.
- Repeat the previous step many times and gradually increase the length of time you leave your dog in the crate and the length of time you go elsewhere.
- After several days, your dog should be able to sit quietly inside the crate for about half an hour with you mostly out of sight. Then, you can start leaving him crated when you are away for a short time. This step can take several days or weeks.

Step 4: Crating Your Dog When You Leave

When your dog is used to staying inside the crate for half an hour without being anxious or afraid, you can leave him in there for a short period of time when you leave the house.

- Put him in the crate using the command you used previously and give him a treat. I suggest you leave some safe toys in there with him as well so he can entertain himself while you are away.
- Try to vary the moment for your "getting ready to leave" routine when your dog is in the crate. While your dog should not be crated for a long period of time before you leave, you can still put them in there between five to twenty minutes before leaving.
- Do not make your departure longer than it should, let alone emotional. It should be short and simple. Praise your dog and give him a treat for entering the cage. Then leave quietly.

When you finally arrive home again, your dog will be super excited. I understand that it's adorable to see him barking and jumping around because he is showing how much he missed you. However, for the sake of your pooch, I advise against rewarding your dog by reflecting their enthusiasm. Doing so will make him anxious over when you will arrive home. Instead, keep your arrivals low-key. Moreover, your dog may start to associate crating with being left alone at this stage. To counter this, continue to crate your dog for short periods now and again when you are home.

Step 5: Crate your Dog at Night

When your dog is comfortable sleeping in his crate at night close to you, you can start to move the crate gradually to somewhere you prefer. Of course, I would still suggest having your dog as close as possible because even when you two are sleeping, being close to each other strengthens the bond between you and your pet.

As the dog gets more comfortable, you can start to move the crate gradually to somewhere you want. Of course, I still recommend placing the crate somewhere as close as possible because even when you two are sleeping, being close to each other strengthens the bond between you and your pet. Another practical benefit is the fact that, just in case your dog needs to go again for some reason, you can hear his whining and let him out on time.

Other Things You Need to Know

Of course, crate training is not as simple as I have pointed out. There are plenty of complications along the way that can confuse even veteran dog owners.

Whining

This is a common issue many dog owners face. If your dog whines or cries while he is inside the crate, it can mean two things. It can be that he wants to be let out, so he can do his business. Orthat he wants to test you and see if you can open the crate to let him out, for no reason. The latter is not desirable as opening the crate and letting him out are perceived as a reward, encouraging him to do it again in the future. If you have followed the training above and gotten the results as described, then your dog should stop whining after a while if you ignore him.

If the whining continues after you have ignored your dog for several minutes, then perhaps he really needs to go. If he responds and becomes excited, take him outside so he can do his business. This should be brief because this is not playtime. If you know for sure that your dog is just testing you, ignore him until the whining stops. I understand how heart-wrenching it is to hear that pitiful whine. I too have had to steel my resolve many times when my new dogs do this to me. However, never give in to their whining. If you do, you will end up teaching your dog to whine loud and long just to get what they want. I had an unpleasant experience with one of my dogs when I was young. The amount of time it took to crate train her again was ridiculous.

If you have gone through the training steps properly without rushing, you should not encounter this problem too often. If this goes out of hand and becomes unbearable and unmanageable, I suggest you start over.

Separation Anxiety

Separation anxiety occurs when your dog becomes too attached to you and becomes very stressed when left alone. It is a lot worse than whining when you leave or a bit of house destruction when you are out. It is so serious that some dog owners become frustrated with their dogs and give them up.

It is no use trying to remedy this problem using the crate. While it may prevent your dog from destroying the house while you are gone, he is prone to injuring himself in a desperate attempt to escape. Not only will your dog be hurt, but he may start to associate the crate with isolation, which ruins your crate training progress. Such a problem requires counterconditioning and desensitization procedures. I recommend that you consult a professional animalbehavior specialist for help. However, you can still use the crate to help your dog to get comfortable being alone if he has not developed separation anxiety. I recommend you start practicing this as soon as you get your dog. I will cover this in chapter 9.

What To Avoid

We have previously discussed these, but here they are again for your convenience:

- Do not rush crate training. It is frustrating to go slow, true, but you need to be sure that the crate is a place where your dog is genuinely happy to stay in.
- Do not yell or pound on the crate if your dog is whining. This is counterintuitive because your dog will not be as eager to enter the crate.
- Do not give in when your dog is whining or his behavior worsens. Your dog can throw a tantrum, and you do not want to reinforce such negative behavior by giving him what he wants.
- Do not use the crate as a form of punishment. Again, you want your dog to associate the crate as a safe haven so that theyare comfortable staying in there.

Chapter 5: Potty Training

To make it clear from the start, house training and potty training are similar. After crate training, housetraining is yet another thing you need to do to familiarize your dog with his new home. The entire success of house training relies on consistency, patience, and positive reinforcement. You need to instill good habits and build a loving, meaningful bond with your dog

The training process should take you between four to six months, but certain dogs may need up to a year. The dog's size can help determine how long it will take. For example, smaller breeds have smaller bladders as well as higher metabolisms. This requires them to go outside more frequently to take care of business. That means they will get to do house training more frequently, resulting in quicker success. Your dog's past experience and living conditions may also be another predictor. You may need to help your dog break old habits before establishing more desirable ones.

Another thing worth mentioning is that setbacks are to be expected. Do not be discouraged by these. So long as you continue to maintain a management program that includes taking your dog out at the first sign that they need to go and offering them a reward, they will learn eventually.

When to Begin?

Experts recommend that you start house training when your dog is between twelve to sixteen weeks old. By then, he can control his bladder and bowel movement well enough to learn how to hold it in.

If your dog is older than twelve weeks when you bring him home and he has been eliminating in his crate (probably even eating his waste), then house training might take longer. If so, you need to reshape the dog's behavior again through encouragement and reward.

Housetraining Steps

If you have followed the crate training steps I have previously highlighted, then you are already one step ahead in housetraining. The first step is to confine your dog to a defined space such as a crate, room, or using a leash. This teaches your dog that he needs to go outside to do his business because he will not soil anywhere near where he will remain for the next hour or so. From there, you can start to introduce him to more and more space in the house where he can roam.

Follow these steps when you start to housetrain your dog:

- Keep his eating schedule precise and regular. Take away his food between meals. Your dog needs to know when exactly they should eat.

- Take your dog out to eliminate first thing in the morning, then once every 30 minutes to an hour, and last thing before he sleeps. Make sure to take him out after meals or after he wakes up from a nap.
- Whenever you take your dog out, make sure to take him to the same spot all the time. His scent from the past will prompt him to go at a precise spot.
- Until your dog is housetrained properly, stay with him outside.
- After your pooch eliminates outside, give him praise or a treat. Since you are already outside, a short walk around the neighborhood is not a bad idea for a reward.

Using a Crate to Housetrain a Dog

A crate can also be used to housetrain your dog at the start. It allows you to keep an eye on him and see when he starts to show signs that he needs a trip to the bathroom. It also serves to teach your dog to hold it in because he does not want to soil his own den. Eventually, he will learn to wait until you let him outside.

Here are a few guidelines for using a crate:

- Make sure the crate is large enough for your dog. He should be able to stand up, turn around, and lie down in it. It should not be so big that he can use one corner as a bathroom.
- If you use the crate for more than two hours at a time, make sure that your dog has access to fresh water. So, put a dispenser in there. This is also another reason why you should use a metal crate because you can easily attach a dispenser.
- Using a crate is a bad idea if your dog eliminates in it. It could mean many things. Your dog may have bad habits from the shelter or pet store where he came from; he may not be let outside enough; the crate could be too big; he could be too young to hold it in.

Tips for Potty Training

Other than what I have described above, there are seven more suggestions you should take into consideration to increase your chance of success.

Keep to a Single Spot

As I have mentioned at the start of the chapter, potty training requires consistency. So, before you start potty training, think of where you want him to go outside the house. It should be the only spot he will go to for the rest of his life, so think carefully. Do you have a yard? Perfect. Take him to a place where he can get to quickly from the door. If you live in an apartment, make sure that there is a natural, easy-to-access ground that is not in the way of foot traffic or that of cars.

After determining where you want your dog to go, make sure to take him there every time he wants to do his business. A dog can smell his territory, so he already knows exactly where if you just show him the way. Rinse and repeat and habit will guide your dog to the same spot without fail. Consistency is important here.

Learn the Signs

Because dogs do not speak our language, they have other means to communicate. They always show visible signs of when they need to go to the bathroom. Thankfully, they are not shy to show that, so you can easily tell if your dog needs a trip to the bathroom if you keep an eye out for them. Take your dog outside immediately to his potty spot if you notice any of the following behaviors:

- Smelling his rear
- Walking in circles
- Barking or scratching at the door (the one that leads to his potty spot)
- Sniffing the floor
- Squatting

If you see the last sign, it may be a bit too late. Still, be ready to open the door anyways so your dog knows that he can go to his usual spot now. Chances are that he will make it in time before he goes in the wrong place.

You need to take your dog outside when you see any of these signs. Therefore, try to plan ahead around your dog's behavior. I suggest keeping a leash at the door, so you can put it on your dog and get him out as quickly as possible. After learning where his bathroom is, he will go to that same spot on his own. Just make sure that you take him to the same spot every time your dog needs to relieve himself.

Keep Meal Time Consistent

When you are potty training your dog, make sure to keep all meal and snack times properly scheduled. This is useful for two main reasons. First, scheduled meals will teach your dog when he can expect to eat throughout the day. Second, if you are feeding your dog at specific times, he should have a precise time when he needs to visit the bathroom. So, you can bring him to his bathroom soon after mealtimes.

Water Bowl

If your dog drinks a lot of water, he may need to go out more frequently. To prevent accidents, make sure to take your dog outside shortly after he drinks water during the potty training process. That way, your dog can be in the right place at the right time.

Go Outside Often

If you want to ensure that your dog takes care of business outside, you need to take him outside regularly as well. As previously mentioned, take your dog outside:

- First thing in the morning;
- Last thing before bed;
- Once every thirty minutes to one hour throughout the day (especially for young dogs); and
- After all feeding and drinking (within thirty minutes).

You can lengthen the time between trips outside until you are confident that your dog will hold it in and let you know when he needs to go outside. Getting your dog to take care of business before bedtime is a good idea as well. Your 3 a.m. self will be grateful for it. I personally dread having to wake up at odd hours just to get the dog outside.

Praise Often

Everyone likes to be told that they are doing a good job, especially for your good boy. This is a positive reinforcement approach that will help your dog in the housetraining process. I recommend you start with giving your dog treats for every successful "business" taken care of, and gradually moving to saying a simple "good job" followed up with some pats. Whatever you do, just make sure your dog knows that you appreciate his efforts to do things the right way.

Address Accidents Calmly

Throughout the potty training program, your dog can and will cause an accident, especially during the early stage. Whenever that happens, be calm and address the situation properly. All you need to do is redirect your dog outside to his potty spot immediately. Remember that accidents tend to occur during the training process anyway. Be patient and never give up. Do not punish your dog because it will only worsen the situation and result in more accidents at home. Some dog owners I have worked with told me that they got so upset whenever their dogs eliminated inside their home that they shoved their dogs' noses into the feces. Let me tell you, it never ends well for both the owners and the dog, because it only makes things worse.

If you happen to catch your dog in the act, clap loudly to tell him that he has done something wrong. Then, take him outside gently by the collar or call him. After he is done, praise him or give him a small treat. While you are outside, it is worth staying there with your dog longer. He may take the time to explore the area so he can go there on his own next time.

After an accident, make sure you clean up the area as quickly and as best as possible. It is important that the place remains spotless and scentless so no further accidents can occur in the same place. You see, if your dog smells his urine or feces in a spot, he will think that it is fine to relieve himself there. You do not want that to happen. As long as your dog knows where his bathroom is, he will have fewer problems. When you clean up the soiled spot, make sure you use pet-safe cleaners and keep your dog well away from the area as it dries up. I highly recommend you clean up using enzymatic cleanser rather than an ammonia-based cleaner to minimize odors that might attract your dog to commit the same mistake again.

Accidents are common in dogs up to a year old. There are many reasons for the accident. Perhaps the housetraining is not complete. Maybe the dog is still unfamiliar with his environment. Just keep on training your pooch. However, if the training seems to have no effect, I suggest you visit the vet just in case he has a medical issue that needs to be addressed. Frequent urinating or defecating in the house can be a symptom of a larger issue. In most cases, they might suggest a simple change to your training routine or a change to his food. However, if it is something serious, you will be glad that you called sooner rather than later.

Preparing for Various Situations

There are many situations that you should be prepared for during the potty training process. Below are some of the scenarios you need to be ready for:

Traveling with a House Training Dog

Raising a dog is a big responsibility, but that does not mean your entire life needs to revolve around him. You may be tempted to take a road trip to an exciting place, and that is completely fine. If you decide to go somewhere far, do not let your dog drag you down. You just need to decide if you want to take your dog with you or not.

If you want to take your pooch with you, then you need to take him outside before you leave and stop once every couple hours to let your dog do his business. You and your passengers do not want to put up with the odor of dog urine or worse, during the whole trip.

If you decide notto take your dog with you, which makes your trip much simpler, then make sure to let whoever is looking after your dog know that he is in the middle of potty training. Give them step-by-step and clear instructions on how you have been working with your dog so far. That way, the other person can keep the training consistent. Your entire progress will be ruined by an inconsistent training program.

Planning for Bad Weather

You will need to deal with bad weather during your dog's potty training phase eventually, so be prepared for it. If it is raining, you cannot expect your dog to hold it in until the sky clears. So, have a large umbrella handy. I suggest putting it close to the door, next to the leash. I suggest you have a towel to wipe off his feet after he takes care of business. You do not want to have mud all over your floor. If it is snowing outside, your new dog may be curious about this new white thing all over the ground. It is fine if curiosity gets the best of your dog. He can explore and play in it a little. Still, he can get cold just like us, so you should usher him to his usual spot as soon as possible. If it is covered in snow, you should grab a shovel and clear out a path for him so he can relieve himself in a more familiar surrounding. We want to be consistent when training your dog.

Moving

If you plan to move within a year or two, I recommend you hold off adopting a dog because it will be too tedious to retrain your dog in your new home. However, if you have already committed to adopting a new dog, and you need to move, keep in mind that your dog will want to explore his new surroundings. The act of moving itself is also stressful for him. In his new home, he may try to mark his new territory with his urine, which may also mark his bathroom location. It is better if you help him decide where his bathroom is, so take him to the spot where you want him to do business just like you did back at your previous location. It is important to get this out of the way as soon as you move in. Take your dog frequently to this spot and reward him if he relieves himself there. This is to reestablish his positive association with good behavior. If your dog has already been housetrained successfully before you move, then the retraining process should be quick. Just make sure you follow the same housetraining routine.

After moving, I recommend you restrict your dog to a certain portion of your house first before gradually introducing him to new areas after he becomes more familiar with his new bathroom routine. You do not want to find a nasty surprise at the other end of your house to which you did not know he had access.

Whatever you do, make sure that your furry friend remains calm during the entire ordeal. An excited, scared, or stressed dog may cause accidents in the home, no matter how well-trained he is.

Chapter 6: The Fundamental Commands

In this chapter, we will discuss the essential skills your dog needs to pick up. Some of these include crate training, potty training, and other basic commands. We have covered the first two. These fundamental commands set the foundation for more complicated commands to teach your dog, should you wish to do so.

There are a few things you need to know before you start teaching your dog:

- Be patient
- Be consistent, both for commands and rewards
- Do not push your dog too hard at the start
- Find somewhere quiet to train your dog, far away from distractions
- Make the learning sessions short and simple
- Make your training consistent and regular
- Do not punish your dog, in any circumstances
- Start by practicing at home or backyard first before exercising commands publicly
- Reward your dog after each successful trick or command
- Show your dog what you want him to know – do not use force
- Time is of the essence – teach your dog a new command as soon as he learns the previous one properly
- Spice things up – make the training fun and entertaining
- Get involved in the training exercise with the dog – he needs someone to play with as well

With that out of the way, let's go over the five main commands your dog needs to know.

The 5 Commands

Keep in mind that your dog needs to learn basic discipline and respect. Both of these will depend on the energy and direction that you give to your dog. Discipline keeps your dog focused so he can learn new tricks and commands quickly.

Other than that, remember that any of the commands I will show you here, if applied appropriately, can be entertaining for both you and your dog. This is ideal as dogs learn much faster if they are also having fun.

"Sit" Command

To teach this command, put the dog treat close to your dog's nose so he can smell it better. Then, move the treat higher up. Your dog should follow the treat, but make sure you move it high enough so he cannot catch the treat. Your dog should sit down so he can pull his head high to follow the treat. The moment his rear touches the ground, say "Sit" and give him the treat and some pats. Rinse and repeat until your dog learns to properly execute this command.

This is a necessary command because you can use it to prevent your dog from doing anything annoying such as getting into trouble with other dogs in the street, or jumping on people when you are taking him for walks. With this command, your dog will sit and not move from his position. You can teach another command such as "Okay" or "Brake" to tell the dog that he can get up now.

"Stay" Command

This command is an upgrade from "Sit." Start by having your dog sit and put a treat close to his nose. Then, give him the "Stay" command. From there, take a few steps back from your dog. If he remains in the same sport, give him a treat. If not, say "No" and move away from him again. That way, he will come to understand that "No" means that he is doing something wrong.

Repeat this exercise several times daily, particularly if you own a hyper-energetic dog. This command challenges your dog to practice self-control, which is crucial.

"Down" Command

This can be a tricky command because it challenges the dog to put itself in a passive or submissive position. It challenges your dog's pack hierarchy.

To teach this command, grab some delicious treats and hold them in a closed hand. Move said hand close to your dog's nose so he can smell it. As he does that, move your hand to the floor. Your dog should have his nose glued to your hand at this point. From there, move your hand along the floor slowly, away from your dog, so he follows your hand until he lays down on his stomach. The moment he does that, say "Down" and give him the treat.

Repeat this exercise every day. In case your dog tries to grab the treat forcefully, retract your hand quickly and say "No." Try again until he executes the command successfully before giving him the treat. Tell the dog to get up with "Okay" or "Brake."

"Come" Command

To teach this command, start by putting a collar and a leash on your dog then take a few steps back from him. Then, ask him to "come" towards you and pull on the leash gently. The moment he approaches you, give him a treat so he knows that this is an exercise.

You need to repeat this exercise many times daily. Release your dog with an "Okay" or "Yes" and show him your affection.

This command helps protect your dog by preventing him from getting into trouble with other dogs. If he runs away in the streets or chasing something or someone, you can get him back using this command.

"No" Command

This command is very useful because you can use it to keep your dog away from improper behavior or dangerous objects at home, street, or anywhere else to protect him from harm.

Start by placing a treat on the ground and keep the dog leashed as you walk slowly toward the treat. The moment your dog becomes interested in the treat and tries to grab it, give the "No" command and pull the dog slightly, just enough to prevent him from grabbing the treat. When he approaches you instead and looks at you, give him a treat and say, "Yes." Rinse and repeat daily and your dog should understand the command.

Chapter 7: The Training Setting for Efficiency and Effectiveness

In this chapter, we will discuss how you can change the training setting to make your training efficient and effective.

As a general rule, you will want to start training your dog in a distraction-free environment. Toget your dog's full attention, remove any toys, and suppress any possible sounds coming from the outside. With your dog's undivided attention, your training will be much more efficient. However, just as how 12 years of school and at least 4 more years of college fail to prepare us for the professional life, training your dog in a quiet environment is not going to be enough. The purpose of the quiet room is to get your dog to understand what he needs to do when he hears the command.

From there, you want to work on changing up the environment by bringing in distractions such as the addition of toys, noises, and the location where you practice. The idea is to simulate the real situation in which your dog can apply what he learns in a controlled environment. Start in a quiet room and move to a more public place such as the park to practice each command. Practice only one command at a time and always start in a quiet room when you teach your dog a new command.

About Equipment

It does not matter as much what equipment you use to train your dog. Positive reinforcement uses very few tools yet achieves excellent results. Other punitive training techniques tend to, more often than not, harm your dog both psychologically and physically. For instance, prong, choke, and shock collars are very popular tools that dog owners and some dog trainers use. The damage they cause to the dog's neck, spine, and internal organs is not a laughing matter. Think what it would feel like if you were choked halfway to death just because you failed to follow a command. If that is unpleasant for you, then it certainly is unpleasant for your dog.

Some salespeople will have you know that such equipment, especially electric fences, do not cause pain when used correctly. I seriously doubt that. Think about it. How can such equipment that is intended to harm your dog to teach him something not cause pain? Of course, it will cause pain, and it will continue to do so several times if you continue to use it. Morally, it is wrong. Practically, it does not work.

From a medical perspective, the anatomy of your dog's neck is similar to yours. Therefore, when pressure is applied by a choke collar or prong, there is a risk of causing thyroid problems, breathing problems, and heart issues.

Thankfully, there are many collars, harnesses, and leashes out there that are comfortable and perfectly safe for you to use without compromising their effectiveness. Such equipment includes No-Pull Harness, or Double Leash, both of which are effective in preventing pulling from your dog when he sees a squirrel looking at him funny.

Choosing a Dog Trainer

Finding the right dog trainer is just as important as choosing the right puppy or dog for you and your family. You see, dog training is not only about your dog. It is also about you. The entire purpose is to teach you the skills you need to know to communicate effectively with your dog, which you will use to teach your dog skills.

Dogs are always learning, whether we are actively teaching them or not. They always try to learn new behaviors and try them out to see what works and what does not. Training gives us the ability to let our dogs know exactly that by rewarding them for their desirable behaviors, and not doing so for those that are not. Moreover, positive reinforcement training helps create and strengthen the bond between you and your dog, as well as ensuring that your dog will respond consistently to your commands.

It just so happens that I'm the perfect candidate for this job. Call me. ☺

I was joking. There are plenty of talented dog trainers out there.

The point is that the dog trainer you choose also uses positive reinforcement training techniques. Positive reinforcement users always use treats, attention, toys, or praise as a form of reward, and the lack thereof as a form of punishment. Positive reinforcement training leads to reliable behavior in dogs through rewards, which is massively more effective. Training would be more stressful and harmful for your dog if he has to work to avoid a correction, which would mean harm for him. However the dog trainer wishes to approach training, the program must not involve yelling, choking, shaking the scruff, tugging on the leash, alpha rolling (by forcing the dog to lay on his back), or other activities that frighten or inflict pain.

Where to Find a Dog Trainer?

Your friends and neighbors is a good place to start as they should have previous experience with a dog trainer. Other than that, check with your vet, local human society, or dog groomer for recommendations.

Keep in mind though that a trainer's membership in a dog trainers association does not mean that he is a suitable instructor. Different associations have different membership criteria, so it is worth checking those out to see if they meet your expectations. Other than that, since no government agency regulates or licenses trainers properly, you must investigate the dog trainer's qualifications before enrolling your pooch in his class. Ask him to explain his training methods, how many years of experience he has, and how he was educated. Make sure to ask him for references from previous clients.

Best Class Format

There are two formats here. Group classes and private classes. Group classes encourage your dog to learn to interact with his fellow dogs, accept handling by other people, and respond to his owner even when distractions are present. You also get to learn how other people interact with their dogs and may benefit from the camaraderie. Private classes are beneficial as well if your dog is shy or if you feel intimidated or prefer working alone. Private lessons are a good idea if you are busy and need the trainer to work around your schedule, not the other way around.

What Constitutes a Good Group Class?

Good trainers will always use positive reinforcement and the best training supplies to maximize training effectiveness. That usually means an ordinary dog collar and leash rather than a choke chain or other harsh methods. A front-leash attachment harness is a good sign that the trainer knows his stuff. Also, ask if you can observe a group class before you sign up. There is hardly any better proof of qualification other than seeing the trainer in action yourself. Keep an eye out for the following:

- Is class size limited to allow for individual attention?
- Are there separate classes for puppies and adult dogs?
- Are there different class levels (such as beginner, intermediate, and advanced)?
- Are training equipment and methods humane?
- Does the trainer use different methods to satisfy different dogs' needs?
- Is proof of vaccination required?
- Are the dogs and their owners, as students, enjoying themselves?
- Are the dogs and owners actively encouraged?
- Is praise given frequently?
- Are voice commands given in an energetic and positive tone?
- Are lesson handouts available?
- Is the information available on how dogs learn, basic grooming, problem-solving, and relation?

Cost

Training costs will be different from trainer to trainer, location, and type of instruction. Of course, if you answer yes to all of the above questions, then the trainer is a perfect candidate and is worth every penny. Private lessons may cost you from $25 to $85 an hour. Group lessons start around $50 for several weeks of sessions. Certain animal shelters offer subsidized training programs. The cost here ranges between $25 to $125, and the class spans over several weeks. The price, of course, depends on whether you adopted your dog from the shelter as well as the number of class sessions in the training program.

Chapter 8: The Clicker

In this chapter, we will discuss clicker training. Clicker training utilizes a clicker, which is a device that produces a distinct sound, a click, to communicate to your dog that he has done something right and that a reward is coming his way. Clicker training falls under positive reinforcement training because you need to reward your dog for proper behavior. It is effective mainly because the sound is unique, so your dog will not be distracted with familiar sounds in busy places. The clicker you hold produces the click that your dog will know immediately. The only difference from other training techniques is the use of the clicker to mark the exact moment when your dog performed the desired behavior. You simply "mark" the behavior with the click, followed up by the reward. Other training methods use different cues such as "Good boy!"

How Does This Work?

Clicker training works around the click sound, which is used to signify that the desired behavior has been achieved and that a reward is coming. Your dog will remember this distinct click early on thanks to its uniqueness. However, some dogs may be startled by the loud click, so I recommend you attempt to suppress the sound by either hiding the clicker in your pocket or wrap a towel around it. Your dog will eventually come to recognize and become fond of the sound.

So, whenever your dog does what he is asked, such as sit or lie down, you press the clicker to produce the click and then follow up with a reward immediately. This gives your dog instant feedback and reinforces the action, choice, or behavior he has just done. Your dog will eventually associate the click with something good (e.g. treats), and he will respond quickly in anticipation of receiving similar rewards in the future.

The clicker is a handheld device, which can be difficult for people to hold. However, you can get a bracelet attachment around the wrist, so it makes things a lot more convenient. You can leave your hands free to hold on a leash. Other people prefer using simple words to mark behaviors such as "Good" or "Yes" in addition to the clicker, so one marks the behavior, and the other signifies a reward. Using both verbal cues and the clicker helps you transition from using the clicker to verbal cues.

How to Use the Clicker

In order to use your clicker, you need to condition your dog to recognize the click as a positive sign. So, do the following:

- Start with some really delicious treats cut into small pieces.

- Whenever you click, give your dog a treat. Do not click and treat at the same time. The treat needs to follow the click, so your dog knows that the click means a treat is coming his way. You can also throw the treat on the ground and click right before your dog eats it.
- Rinse and repeat while you are standing up, sitting down, or moving around and in different kinds of environments. That way, your dog understands that the click, no matter where he hears it, means that he has done something right and will receive a yummy reward.
- Rinse and repeat this exercise a few times a day for a few minutes at a time. You know when your dog is conditioned to recognize the click when he anticipates the treat whenever you click.

Clicker Rules

Other than that, there are a few rules you need to know:

- Click only once
- If you click, you must treat
- Do not use the clicker like a remote control. Do not point it at your dog when you click. Hold the clicker at your side or behind your back whenever you click.
- If your dog is scared of the click, muffle the sound with a towel, get a softer clicker, or use another teaching method.

Teaching Your Dog to Sit

This is an example of training using the clicker. Other training using this device should follow the same patterns:

- Catch your dog in the act of sitting. The moment his rear touches the ground, click and treat.
- Rinse and repeat whenever you see him sitting. As he starts to sit, say "Sit," and click and treat when he sits.
- When your dog understands the meaning of the command "Sit," you can ask him to perform the action.
- Ask your dog to "sit."
- The moment your dog puts his rear on the ground, click and follow up with the treat immediately.

As you can see, there are two main phases in training your dog using the clicker. You need to mark the behavior with a clicker first before you attach the command. From there, you can start to phase out the click as your dog becomes more proficient. The next step is phasing out both the click and treat.

When you reward your dog intermittently, you are practicing variable positive reinforcement. You want to train your dog to the point that he is able to respond when you don't have to click or treat. The only way to reach that stage is through regular, constant, and consistent practice. The end result is your dog sitting whenever you say "Sit," and the reward for him is a simple pat or praise.

You should practice only one command at a time until your dog reaches this stage before you move on to another command, following the same process. Through such training, you can teach so many commands to your dog.

Chapter 9: Dealing with Negative Behavior

A dog's behavior is more complex than we think. It is deeply rooted in how he is bred, socialized, and trained. While the first factor, breed, is well outside our control, we retain two-thirds of the power over how our dogs behave. Yours may be sociable and confident, so he is able to cope in our world and respond to different cues properly. This is only possible if you take the time to teach him basic cues and recognize the difference between minor inconvenient behaviors and more serious behavioral problems as he grows. With time and effort, you can curb many behavioral problems from happening early on through positive reinforcement training.

Basic cues are more than just ensuring that your dog behaves properly. They should be entertaining to your dogas well. After all, you don't want to attend a boring class, but you will never miss one that makes hours seem like seconds. The same should apply to your dog. You should perform dog training in a way that he can enjoy. Not only is it more effective, but it also helps build the communication between you and provides all the important dog education foundation you need if you want to curb serious unwanted behaviors such as aggression as your dog grows up.

You see, dealing with dog behavior does not need to be all serious all the time. You are teaching your dog behaviors that would benefit him. You are not training him to fight in a war. So, have fun with him while teaching him tricks. You can even take the training to a whole new level by participating in a dog sport.

Making training fun and educational is the core of addressing and curbing undesirable behaviors. When it comes to the don'ts of curbing negative behaviors, NEVER force your dog into proper behaviors through confrontational techniques. You can only have a happy, well-behaved dog through force-free training methods.

Preventing Barking

We have all experienced this problem. Maybe your dog is barking at a passing squirrel… at 3 in the morning. Occasional barking is fine. We cannot expect our dog to be silent all the time. It is only when he starts to bark all the time that we need to do something about it. You certainly are not alone if you have this problem. It is one of the most common complaints many dog owners have. To make matters worse, this is a problem that can be difficult to solve. So, why do dogs bark?

Step 1: Why Dogs Bark

There are so many reasons why your dog barks. Barking is a natural form of communication for dogs, after all. To stop him from barking, you need to first understand why he does that in the first place. By identifying the root cause, you can work to eliminate or minimize its influence. In some cases, the cause is within plain sight. Maybe there is a squirrel that frequents your backyard. In this scenario, your dog barks to alert you of an intruder or noise. This is one major reason why dog owners want a dog in their home. They function as a super cute and reliable alarm. If you hear this kind of barking at 3 in the morning, then there may be something that is worth your attention. Hopefully, though, there will not come a time when you hear it.

In other cases, your dog barks at you to gain your attention because he wants something such as food or affection. Whatever the case may be, it will take some practice to make that barking habit go away, and when he does bark, you know that something is up and requires your immediate attention. Until a better behavior is taught, your dog will bark when he receives the same stimulus. In some cases, your dog just barks because he is bored. If this is the case, then the solution is very simple. You just need to give him more exercise, both physically and mentally, and his barking behavior should go away.

Step 2: Not Reward Barking

As with anything in positive reinforcement training, the only form of punishment is not giving a reward. The same applies here. You need to deny your dog any form of reward for his barking. If you reward him, whether intentional or not, it will reinforce his behavior. In fact, your attention is rewarding enough for your dog. If you go over to check what he is barking at, or you just shout at him, that is also rewarding. To make matters worse, if you continue to reward your dog this way, his behavior will worsen over time because he knows that barking gets a reaction. So, he will continue to bark to get your attention. So, this is how you should approach the problem:

- If your dog is barking for attention, turn, and walk away. Only give your dog what he wants when he is quiet.
- If your dog barks when he wants food, leave the kitchen. Return only when he has stopped.
- If your dog is barking to go outside, wait until he is quiet before opening the door. The exception is, of course, when he needs to "go."
- If your dog barks at someone walking by your house, don't call him until he is quiet.

Doing the above should be enough to stop your dog from barking for attention, especially if you reward him for doing the right thing instead. The only problem is that barking itself can be self-reinforcing. For instance, if your dog barks at the mailman to go away, the act of the postman leaving is perceived as a reward. This reinforces the barking even though you ignore your dog. In such situations and for most types of alert barking, you may need to instill an alternative behavior into your dog.

Step 3: Training an Alternative Behavior

When you have determined the reason behind your dog's barking and eliminated the reward your dog would get from his behavior, the next step is to give him an alternative behavior. Your dog should switch over to the alternative and desirable behavior fairly quickly if he believes that he is getting a better reward if he behaves differently.

So, start by listening for exactly the moment when your dog barks. Does he start barking the moment he hears footsteps outside or does he wait until the person is right outside the door? You want to find your dog's tolerance level here. Some dogs bark the moment they see something. Others wait until it passes a certain boundary before they sound the alarm. From there, you can start to teach your dog a different behavior that gets him a reward. The alternative behavior should interrupt the undesired one before your dog reaches his barking threshold.

When your dog sees or hears the trigger and before he starts barking, ask him to perform a behavior that you want. You can ask him to sit, lie down, or just look at you. This will take his eyes off whatever it is that triggers him. When you have successfully interrupted him, give your dog a treat and a lot of praise. If you miss the trigger and your dog starts barking, don't interrupt him because that is rewarding your dog for barking. Instead, just ignore him and wait for the next opportunity. If possible, I recommend you have someone create the trigger so you can practice. Of course, you cannot always practice all the time as you cannot be with your dog constantly when someone walks by. This practice is great for noise triggers because your dog often hears people coming way before seeing them, so repeat this process as often as possible. It is time-consuming, true, but your dog will eventually understand what you want him to do when faced with a certain trigger. Another thing to keep in mind is that your dog may bark with a hint of fear in his voice. Observe your dog's facial expression to determine his fear or anxiety threshold and interrupt his behavior before he gets too anxious. It would be too late already if your dog starts getting stressed or anxious.

Step 4: Preventing Reinforcement

Finally, you need to remove the trigger or at least minimize its influence on your dog by keeping him away to avoid reinforcement whenever you cannot train your dog. This could mean keeping him inside with you rather than letting him run loose in the garden. You can confine him to a certain room at the back of the house or anywhere away from the trigger if it happens at a certain point in time, i.e. the postman's visit. If you have crate-trained your dog, then keeping him in his own crate is a great idea to contain him to one spot. You can also take a more direct approach to solving the problem by removing it so that your dog has no reason to bark. If your dog has a habit of barking at people at the fence, I recommend blocking his vision through the fence by building a higher fence that does not allow visibility through.

What Not to Do

As always, there are common pitfalls that dog owners commit when they attempt to teach their dogs to stop barking at literally everything. One of which is shouting or physically hurting their dog. This is never a good solution for any unwanted behavior. Other than ruining the owner/pet relationship, such harsh methods will create negative associations. Even if your dog does not bark, he will be stressed and can become aggressive the next time he is in the same situation.

Preventing Biting

Biting is a particularly annoying behavior, as I am certain many dog owners will agree. Knowing how to stop dogs from biting requires patience from both the dog and the owner. Neglecting this problem can lead to a chewed chair leg or a demolished sandal. Some owners may defend that dogs are just teething or this is just how dogs explore and understand the world. They may be right, but chewing is still annoying, especially when it results in the destruction of your good shoes.

It is true dogs use their teeth to explore the world in addition to their eyes, ears, and nose. They primarily use their mouth to play, explore, and teeth all the time. Your dog's teeth are super sharp because they are carnivores. Anyone who has been nipped by a puppy will understand how sharp the teeth are, let alone getting one from a dog.

Dogs play using their mouths all the time, but when they start to bite each other, one will start to feel the pain. This often ends up with the injured dog retaliating, which can quickly lead to a fight, or retreating hastily from the responsible dog. This is when your dog learns bite inhibition to understand social etiquette. Dogs should learn about bite inhibition at an early age already if theyhave been properly socialized. However, if they are raised alone and only have humans to play with, then they may miss out on this valuable lesson.

Stopping Dog Bites

The best way to stop your dog from biting you is by doing exactly what a dog would do if he got bitten. Simply stop giving attention to your dog to deny him the reward, and only give it to him when he acts appropriately. From there, you can start to reinforce better alternatives. Here's how:

- Withdraw attention: Your dog needs to learn that when he bites, he won't be getting the good things.
- Positive reinforcement: When he starts to play appropriately, continue playing with him, which is something that he wants.
- Provide an alternative: Take the slipper away from him and give him his own rope chew or toy.

Of course, we all wish it was this straightforward. Stopping a dog from biting may require a deeper understanding of your dog's behavior than what I have pointed out above. For example, you may need to take a different approach to address this problem, especially if he has separation anxiety. You also need to understand bite inhibition, triggers, and types of biting.

Bite Inhibition

Think about the difference between punching someone playfully on the shoulder and punching someone in the face when they have wronged you. What is the difference other than the emotion? Force. Bite inhibition is simply learning how to limit the force and strength of your dog's bite. It tells him that other dogs and humans are not as tough as the table leg he is used to chewing on. Because the only defense for a dog is biting, they need to learn bite inhibition to limit the damage they can do. Every dog can and will bite out of fear and anxiety.

When dogs play together, they chew and nip at each other. This is fine if done lightly. However, when one bites a little too hard, this is when you hear the yelp or squeal. It tells the responsible dog that he bit a little too hard. When this happens, the interaction between the two dogs ends, which means the denial of reward for the responsible dog. Through this trial and error, dogs learn that playtime is over if they bite hard. This is operant learning, which is when your dog learns his lesson the hard way.

So now we understand why learning bite inhibition at an early age is crucial. Dogs that learn how to use their mouth gently are less likely to bite hard and pierce the skin if they ever bite someone out of fear or anxiety.

As previously mentioned, dogs should learn this on their own if they have been properly socialized. If your dog has not received this socialization, then you just need to withdraw attention. Follow the three bullet points above, and your dog should learn eventually.

Rough Play

Normally, I don't recommend playing rough with your pet because it is similar to biting hard. A little rough and tumble is fine, but there is a line you should not cross. Unfortunately, children are the ones who often cross this line. This can cause your dog to panic if he thinks he is being attacked and will retaliate, which can lead to a mess. As with any other training method, teaching bite inhibition requires consistency. Everyone in the house needs to be teaching the dog the same thing.

Rough and tumble is fine, but when your dog starts to mouth on your skin or clothing, end the game then and there. The same goes for tug of war, which is a game I will go over in a later chapter. You want your dog to understand that lively and energetic play is acceptable, so long as biting or mouthing is not in the picture.

What Causes Dogs to Bite

All of us want to see our dogs running around in the dog park and playing and chasing other dogs but, through all of those interactions, your dog may develop aggressive tendencies. Indicators of aggressive intent when biting include a fixed gaze, stiff posture, and a deep tone of growling. There are many reasons why dogs become aggressive. The most common is that it solves the problem. Such animalistic instinct is perfectly understandable because some of us turn to violence to get things done as well. Aggression can come from frustration, guarding (toys, food, etc.), anxiety, and the lack of appropriate socialization. Anxiety and frustration, in particular, can be a result of punishment.

There are a few biting types. Understanding and identifying them is important, so you know what behavior you need to focus on during training. You can break down dogs' bites into four categories:

- Exploration and play
- Aggressive
- Guarding
- Teething

You can tell them apart by studying your dog's body language. If he has that innocent and relaxed look, then he is either exploring or playing. Aggressive or guarding bites are shown with a stiff body, wrinkled face, growling, snarling, and the exposure of teeth. This shows building tension and a bite could follow very soon if you do not tread carefully.

Mouthing, Biting, and Nipping

All of these are completely normal behaviors in dogs. The only problem is that some dogs have the tendency to do some of them excessively, which is why we need to teach them proper behavior, well into their adulthood if need be.

Nipping is light nibbling, occurring regularly during play and exploration. Your dog should exhibit happiness and energy. Mouthing occurs during teething, and you can tell because your dog will be gnawing on something. Biting is self-explanatory and is a behavior displayed by aggressive dogs. We want to control our dog's biting here because it can cause serious, even lethal, injury.

Some General Guidelines

You should take some time off to allow your dog to mingle as soon as possible so he can learn bite inhibition. When he does so, it is much easier for you to teach him to practice restraint. Playtime is just as crucial for your dog as it is for other dogs because he will get to learn social etiquette. Getting him to mingle with other dogs is the best way to teach your dog bite inhibition as he learns from others what is and is not appropriate, both for playing and using teeth. Playing is a great learning opportunity because it is entertaining, making it an ideal situation in which to teach your dog restraint. Here, other dogs are the better teacher. However, if your dog has a nasty habit of biting too hard or too much, you may need to start teaching him at home to reinforce bite inhibition. Here are the general guidelines when you train your dog at home about bite inhibition:

- Stop playing immediately when your dog starts mouthing or biting. Deny him attention (reward) by turning away. After a few seconds, if your dog stops mouthing, you can continue playing with him.

- Say something like "Ow" when your dog bites you. When he stops, give him praise and affection.
- Use the command "gentle" when you give your dog treats and slowly roll out the treat in your hand to him if he is not biting or mouthing.
- Teach your dog the "Off" command so you can get him to take his mouth away from your hand. Whenever he does that, give him a treat.
- Make sure to have some chew toys such as Kongs or Everlasting Treat Balls so your dog can chew on those instead. I advise against using other toys such as soft squeakers or fabric toys because they actually teach your dog that it is acceptable to chew things up, which is counterintuitive.
- Do not clamp his mouth shut or hit him on the nose to punish your dog for biting. It can send him into a fight or flight mode and cause him to bite your hand instinctively.
- Do not tease your dog or try to start playing with your hands.

Preventing Chewing

Almost all the dogs I have worked with love chewing, and this is also quite natural. However, when chewing leads to the destruction of objects in your house, it becomes a problem. That is why chew toys are created for your dog, so he can chew on those instead of your expensive shoes. Chewing can be a recreational activity for your dog, but excessive and destructive chewing can be a sign of a deeper problem such as separation anxiety.

Your dog chews on things to relieve stress. This activity triggers the release of endorphins in your dog's brain, which causes him to feel good. If your dog chews on the door frame or the window, it means he is trying to get out, which is a sign of a behavioral problem. As with any behavioral issue, I suggest you take your dog to the vet first to rule out any possible medical causes that could exacerbate this behavior. Other than that, here are some ways you can stop your dog from chewing:

- No matter what causes your dog to chew excessively, exercise and enrichment are key to changing the desire to chew in your dog. Your dog is energetic, which means he is more likely to indulge in destructive behaviors to burn all of that energy. If he is tired, he will be a happy little dog that does not want to chew excessively.
- Create a dog-proof room (or dog-proof your entire house) or use baby gates to keep your dog in a certain area where you know he cannot cause destruction by chewing when you leave him unsupervised. Just make sure this room in your house is close to the busy areas, so your dog does not feel isolated.
- Give your dog appropriate chew toys to keep him busy. Just make sure that they are durable and safe for your dog even with heavy chewing.

- Find a good outlet for your dog's energy. Taking your dog out for a walk gives him the physical exercise he needs, but he also needs something to work his mind. Play some games with him as I have described above, or give him puzzles or interactive toys to play with.
- If possible, find a sport in which both you and your dog love to do together to release any pent up stress or tension your dog may be feeling.

Preventing Digging

Again, you need to understand why your dog digs in the first place before you begin to address this problem. There are many reasons why your dog digs excessively. Maybe he does it to cover up his waste after he does his business, which is fine. However, when your dog digs without actually going to the bathroom, it could be because he is bored. It is not so bad if he does it in the house because he cannot dig through the floor. However, if he does it in the yard, it could lead to some accident if you do not watch where you are walking.

If your dog has a bad habit of digging up your entire yard, I recommend you examine your dog's day-to-day activities and restructure everything. Other than that, dogs are known to dig to escape the heat. You see, the ground beneath the surface is usually cooler, so they tend to dig up the cool ground to form a cold and comfy bed to sleep in. In this case, the problem can be fixed by simply giving him his own pool.

If your dog digs because he is curious, then the problem is more serious. For example, if your dog sees you digging in your yard, whether to garden or landscape, he will automatically assume that you are trying to hide something under that pile of dirt. Curiosity is a powerful motivator for your dog, so he can and will literally unearth everything to get to the bottom of his question, literally. If he thinks that freedom is on the other side of your fence, he will go right underneath it. If he believes that you are hiding some juicy treats under the flowerbed, well, you won't find a flowerbed there once your dog is done with it. To make matters worse, digging is similar to barking in the sense that it is self-reinforcing because digging is super fun for your dog. This means getting your dog to stop digging is going to be a very difficult task.

If your dog digs excessively, then there is probably an environmental factor that motivates him to so. It can be boredom or the heat. Again, there can be many factors that lead to this behavior. The lack of training is also one of them. Thankfully, there are ten actionable steps you can follow to stop your dog from digging. These are the most effective practices in the dog training world. If you follow every single one of them, your dog should understand that digging is a big no-no.

Give Him a Proper Digging Spot

Just like potty training, the best way to address your dog's excessive digging behavior is by giving him a spot to do so. Because digging is self-reinforcing behavior, you cannot expect your dog to quit digging. So, you might as well embrace his behavior and attempt to control where he can do it to minimize the damage to your yard.

The digging site can be as simple as a kiddie pool or a boxed off area filled with sand or loose dirt. It can even be a specific space in your yard. Stick with what works best for you. If your dog ignores the sandbox you set up for him and goes for the spot underneath the tree, then use the latter as the designated excavation site for your dog.

Keep in mind that curiosity is a very powerful motivator for your dog. You can use it to your advantage by intentionally piquing your dog's interest. You can do so by burying chew bones or toys in the digging site. I recommend that you make sure he sees you burying the good stuff to get his attention and get him to come and investigate. He should come around quickly and start to sniff and dig things up. This is the perfect strategy because digging reinforces his behavior, but it rewards him again by giving him toys. He will believe that the best digging spot will be the dig site because he knows he will find something interesting under the dirt there.

Positive Reinforcement Training

You can further capitalize on double reinforcement by giving your dog praise and some treats when he digs in the designated digging spot. Normally, I recommend rewarding sparingly with treats, but you shouldn't skimp on the treats in this training. The positive reinforcement you give is going to increase your dog's desire to dig exclusively in the spot you gave him. It does not help if your dog digs in his designated area, but also everywhere else to check if there are any goodies to be found. So, you want to convince your dog that this is literally the best spot for him as soon as possible.

Do Not Get Angry

I, for one, always get upset when my dog digs up my pristine backyard. I understand that it can be really hard to not become angry at your dog when he does something that you know he understands he is not supposed to do.

It seems that your dog is taking a defiance stance against you, which can be irritating after all the things you have given him such as food, shelter, etc. In some cases, it is defiance. Most of the time though, it is just boredom or a plea for attention and affection.

Regardless of the reasons, it is important that you do not display anger or aggression toward your dog over the problem. Doing so will only damage the relationship you have worked so hard to create. Instead, be firm and commanding when you confront such behavior, without being violent or imposing.

When you approach your dog without showing any signs of threats, he will respond in kind. However, if your dog thinks you are going to hurt him, he may either flee or bite back. If it is the latter, you can be sure that he will draw blood.

Tire Your Dog Out

Your dog prefers sleeping over digging if he is exhausted. If your schedule does not have sufficient activities to stimulate his mind and body, then consider adding those activities in so that your dog gets enough exercise. At the end of the day, he will be so tired that he will just want to head off to sleep the moment he gets the opportunity to do so. Depending on the dog's breed, you may need to incorporate more or less exercises to prevent your dog from getting bored. If he does get bored, he will use the extra energy to exhibit destructive behavior.

Crate Train

If you have crate-trained your dog, putting him in a crate is a good idea for when you cannot keep an eye on him. He will not dig up and destroy his own den, not that he can anyway. Of course, doing so is only a temporary solution because sitting in a crate is not particularly exciting for your dog, so the excessive energy still needs to be burnt. Consider throwing a few toys in there for your dog while you are away.

Do Not Leave Dogs Unsupervised

Most dogs, even those that like to exercise a lot, do not like it if you leave him outside alone for hours. They will get bored and stressed by external environmental factors such as other dogs' barks. When this happens, your dog will start digging to cope.

Fill the Hole with Waste

You may find this to be unpleasant if you are not used to handling a dog's waste. Still, no one can deny that this is not one of the most effective ways to curb your dog's digging behavior. If he has taken a liking to a particular spot that you do not want him to dig, simply fill the problem spot with his waste. He should avoid those places immediately. Just like us, dogs are hygienic animals, and they do not want to touch their own waste.

You can take it a step further by mixing the waste with water and then water the area you don't want your dog to dig with the feces concoction you just mixed up. Of course, it will make your yard stinky for about a week at most, but your dog is going to smell it for much longer and avoid the area.

Give Your Dog Bonus

At a certain point, you will have to leave your dog unsupervised for an extended period of time. When you do, make sure you reward your dog for waiting for you to keep him busy while you are away. A large bone or puzzle toy should be enough to keep him occupied.

Give Your Dog a Pool

As I have mentioned earlier, dogs sometimes dig to create a hole in which they rest in to escape the heat. German Shepherds are one of those breeds that do not have a high tolerance for heat. But you can provide your dog with a better alternative – a pool. Consider digging a half-full kiddie pool for your dog so they can hop in to chill. It can be any container as long as it is big enough.

Use Plastic Cover Wire Netting

To protect your flower beds or other precious plants, consider getting one of them at the local garden store or plant nursery. It is a great solution to keep your dog off the plant and keep the weed down as well.

Dealing with Separation Anxiety

Separation anxiety plays out in many ways. Your dog may scratch at the door, cry, whine, or bark excessively. He may go to the bathroom in the house or chew on everything he can get his paws on. How can you tell it is a product of separation anxiety? Simple. It happens whenever you leave the house. Other problems such as chewing, digging, barking may occur whether you are present or not. The distinction here is presence.

There are many reasons behind the development of separation anxiety in dogs. To this day, we still do not have a firm grasp on the subject. Whatever the case may be, it is important to keep in mind that the destructive tendency caused by this anxiety is not your dog's fault.

Such behaviors may result from panic or can be used as a coping mechanism, both of which are totally understandable. Many people turn to alcohol or even drugs to cope, so what your dog does is not any different. Therefore, punishing your dog rather than addressing the problem will not solve anything. The best way to approach this problem is to get your dog used to being left alone.

You can help your dog learn to be comfortable being alone by taking some time to follow the pointers below. Start as soon as possible, right after you get your dog.Even if he does not display any signs of separation anxiety,it might already be too late if he starts to show signs of it. By then, you may need to consult a professional.

- Have a specific routine and stick to it. Unlike us, dogs like routine. So, create a schedule for your dog and make sure everyone, including you and everyone else in the house, sticks to it.
- Practice preventative training.
- Make sure your dog takes care of his business before you crate him. He cannot hold it in for that long and forcing him to stay in close proximity to his own feces will only stress him more.

- Crate him for short periods of time when you are around. For instance, if you are watching television or when you are reading, put your dog in his crate and put the crate close to you. Increase the crate time gradually and reward him if he remains calm by giving calm praise.

- From there, start leaving your dog in his crate and go somewhere out of sight. Leave him in his crate unsupervised for a few minutes at a time and then gradually increase the time inside the crate.

- Try to limit the attention your dog gets, and the time it takes you to prepare to leave. Make your exit lowkey if possible. That way, the act of you leaving will not be such a shock to your dog. He may even think that your departure is normal.

- When you finally let your dog out of the crate, remain calm, and try not to overdo your greeting. A little pat should suffice. You don't want to excite him.

- I advise against crating dogs all the time, but that does not mean you should give your dog the whole house to play with. Do not rush freedom. Normally, dogs are not supposed to be left unsupervised until they are at least a year-and-a-half (18 months) or older.

- Try to make sure that there is at least someone in the house. If not possible, consider hiring a dog walker or ask your neighbor to visit him during the day while everyone else is out at work or in school. Make sure that your dog has some company.

- If possible, keep your schedule similar on weekends, so your dog does not get confused when everyone is gone on Monday.

Other Tips

Many dogs cry or whine when you leave them alone for a long time. This is normal. Separation anxiety is characterized by the destructive behavior done by your dog to anything he can get his paws on, as well as constant barking, whining, or inappropriate elimination in his crate or on the carpet, even if you have potty trained him properly. So, it is pretty easy to tell if your dog has separation anxiety. If you cannot resolve this problem on your own, I recommend you seek out professional help.

Other than that, whenever you leave the house, make it uneventful. By making your departure overly emotional with lots of hugs and goodbyes, you may end up increasing your dog's anxiety level. You can give him an interactive toy to keep him occupied while you are gone.

Finally, make your return just as lowkey. Let him out of the crate and take him outside so he can go to the bathroom. Although older dogs can hold it in for longer, it is still a good idea to let him relieve himself. You can let him out, greet, and praise him calmly.

Chapter 10: Have Some Fun!

As I have mentioned many times throughout this book, you can maximize the effectiveness of dog training if you make it fun for both you and your dog. You will both enjoy and look forward to the training session. Other than that, it also helps strengthen your bond. This is what this chapter is all about. Here is a list of games you can use to teach your dog certain behaviors.

Leave It

We are familiar with the command "Leave It," as it is one of the advanced dog commands. This game was pioneered by Sophia Yin, and the purpose of the command and the game is to protect the dog from ingesting dangerous objects or prevent him from chasing or focusing on other distractions as you take him for walks. So, this is what you need to do:

- Have your dog on a leash, and toss a treat just out of his reach.
- Your dog will pull and strain at the leash as he tries to reach the treat. Wait until he gives up and stops. Just before he gives up, give the command "Leave It."
- When he does so, give him a treat for looking at you.
- Only then can you walk toward the treat. Make sure to have a loose leash as you do so.
- Rinse and repeat.

You know that your dog has learned to practice restraint when he stops pulling you toward anything that interests him on walks. To solidify the skill, practice this in a variety of locations.

It's Your Choice

This game teaches your dog to ignore dropped food in the home. This is also a part of the "Leave It" command. If you repeat this game enough times, your dog will learn to wait for your permission to take any food. Here's how you do it:

- Put some tasty treats in your hand and hold your hand close to your dog.
- Keep your hand closed as your dog sniffs, nibbles, or paws at your hand.
- Open your hand only when your dog stops inspecting your hands and sits back to wait.
- Close your hand when your dog tries to grab the treats in your hand.
- The moment he returns back to wait, then wait for a few seconds and then place one treat on the ground.
- Gradually increase the waiting time between opening your hand and giving the treat to your dog, so that he has to watch you open your hand for longer.

- You can also take this game up a notch by putting the food on the floor and covering it with your hand, and then by covering it with your foot. You can add in the command "Leave It" just before you open your hand if you want.

Relax on Your Mat

This is a great game for your dog if you have got yourself a super hyper-energetic breed. Teaching your dog to slow down and relax is crucial. This is how you accomplish this:

- Select a blanket, towel, or mat you want to use. It should not be a dog bed.
- Put the mat on the ground in front of your dog.
- Treat your dog if he shows any interest in the mat, such as looking, moving toward, sniffing, or pawing on it. Keep the treats flowing if your dog remains on the mat.
- From there, start to narrow down on your reward criteria. Try to get to the point when you only reward your dog when he lays down on the mat. It is also okay to skip past the previous step by giving your dog the "Down" command and continue to reward him for every 10 seconds he remains on the mat.
- Once you have solidified this training, try to mix things up and practice in different places and with distractions.

Red Light-Green Light

This game aims to teach your dog polite leash walking skills without the use of treats, although treats can speed up training significantly. You can combine this with the U-Turns, which I will show you next. So, this is how you play Red Light-Green Light:

- Have your dog on a leash. Take him for walks as usual.
- Start walking forward and your dog should take the lead. Make sure you walk slower than your dog. When your dog reaches the end of his leash and starts to pull, stop, and wait. Do not tug on the leash.
- Wait until the leash forms a "J." Then, mark the behavior with a word such as "Good" or "Yes."
- Start walking again.
- Rinse and repeat.

This can take a long time and is particularly frustrating. But it is effective. I suggest you use a flat collar when playing this game and a harness during normal walks.

U-Turn

This technique was developed by Grisha Stewart. The idea is to teach your dog to yield small amounts of pressure on the leash so you can direct him easily. Start inside your home, in a distraction-free room, and have some tasty treats handy. You can use the clicker if your dog still relies on clicker training.

Start by clipping the leash on the collar, and wait until things are calm. Then, apply slight pressure on the leash to one side and wait for your dog to yield a bit to that pressure. He might even move toward the direction of the pressure, or just shift his weight a bit. That is fine. We take what we can get.

Mark the moment when he leans even slightly in that direction and give him a treat. Rinse and repeat until your dog starts to respond readily to very slight leash pressure while inside your home. Then, you can repeat this game outside. From there, gradually increase the number of distractions in the environment while playing this game, so your dog responds to even the slightest leash pressure.

Nosework

This game is intended to tire your dog, so he does not pick up any bad behaviors with the extra energy. Your dog needs to sniff really hard to find delicious, hidden treats. Sniffing helps calm him down as well. Dogs feel right at home when they need to use their nose to sniff out food, and this game caters to their natural instinct. Nosework works well to calm stressed-out dogs. To play this game, do the following:

- Use boxes with treats in them to teach your dog to look for treats using his nose.
- Gradually increase the difficulty of the game by putting the boxes in different configurations, such as behind the couch.
- Start to hide treats outside the boxes.
- Add some vertical complexity such as hiding the treat under the table.
- Try new locations.

Ready, Set, Down

This tug-based game teaches your dog to drop toys on your command, even when he is really excited. When your dog gets excited, it can get very difficult to calm him down. The purpose of this game is to address this problem as it teaches him to listen to you in distracting environments. This is how to play the game:

- First, make sure your dog knows how to play tug of war, how to drop a toy on cue, and how to learn one more behavior.
- Start playing tug with your dog. Just play lightly at first because you don't want him to get super excited right off the bat.

- Give your dog the cue to drop the toy

- Give your dog the cue for him to sit, lie down, or whatever command he is proficient at.

- Reward your dog for listening by restarting the game.

- Restart the game intermittently whenever your dog drops the toy.

- Rinse and repeat. If possible, mix in different cues to make your dog think.

- Work on increasing the intensity of the tug game. However, the moment your dog stops listening to you, reduce the intensity level, and make sure he masters the previous intensity level.

Go Find It

The game is all about asking your dog to find a specific toy. It works really well with dogs that love playing with toys. You can play this game to stimulate your dog's mind, as there are not many ways to do so, to begin with. This game helps to tire your dog out, so he does not pick up undesirable behavior with the excess energy.

- Start with one toy out only. If you don't have a name for the toy already, think of one. Just like commands, the name should be simple. Then, tell your dog to "Go get X" or "Go find X." Whatever command you pick, stick with it. The reward for your dog here is him being able to play with it. Most dogs get what you mean immediately if you say the cue in an excited voice and point at the toy.

- Phase-out the pointing and just use the verbal cue. Continue to reward your dog by playing with the toy.

- From there, you can introduce another toy. The new toys should be a bit less exciting than the toys you named. Only reward your dog when he grabs the correct one.

- Give a name to the second toy by following the first and second steps. This is easier if your dog loves both toys almost equally. If your dog goes crazy for the ball but ignores the squeaky toy, do not use those two toys. Doing so only leads you to failure.

- Repeat the third step with the two named toys and alternate which toy you ask for.

- Gradually increase the number of toys that your dog knows by name.

Smart x50

This game was invented by Kathy Sdao. It focuses on teaching your dog basic life skills and manners around the house.

- Put 50 pieces of treats or dog's dinner kibble, in a jar or a treat pouch.

- Pay careful attention to your dog as you go about your day. Do not give him prompts or cues to do anything specific.

- When your dog does something you like, such as sitting, lying down, looking up at you before going through the door, choosing to ignore the cat, etc. say "Good boy!" and give him a treat.
- Rinse and repeat until the treats are gone.

This is a great exercise as you can capitalize on the good behaviors your dog already displays. It also helps you recognize his desirable behaviors. Finally, this is manageable even in a busy household.

Exchange Games

This game helps to reinforce your dog's "leave it" proficiency. I do not recommend you play this game without the help of a trainer if your dog has issues with sharing, or resource guarding.

- Start by giving your dog a toy that he likes. He should take it into his mouth or play around with it.
- Approach your dog and say "Good boy" or any familiar cue when he looks at you. If you have a clicker, you can click as well. Toss him some delicious treats nearby. He should drop the toy and go for the treat. If he does not, you either need a better treat or a less exciting toy.
- Pick up the toy he had while he is enjoying his snack.
- Give him the toy back.
- Rinse and repeat. The idea is to excite him when you approach him.
- Continue to play this game until your dog drops his toy the moment you come near him.

Look at That

This game is intended to teach your dog to calmly notice everything exciting, scary, or distracting. It is great for leash reactive or aggressive dogs if done properly. If your dog has any problems with these behaviors, it is a good idea to get a dog trainer instead.

- Take treats while you are out walking your dog.
- When you see an object of interest such as a person, dog, cat, or squirrel, click or say "Yes" and feed your dog when he looks back at you.
- If your dog does not turn toward you because he is too interested in the object of focus, you are either too close to the said object or your treats are not good enough. Try to change either of the two next time.
- Move away from the object of interest.

One-Two-Three Walking

This game works very well to help your dog process the environment and learn how to handle distractions. Before you start, have some treats ready, but do not lure your dog around with the treats. Hide them in your pocket or treat pouch.

This game is super simple. Just count "1, 2, 3!" out loud. The moment you say "3," give your dog a treat. Start by delivering the treats right to your dog's mouth until he understands that he gets a treat every time you say 3. From there, start to give the treat right next to the pocket or seam of your pants at head height for your dog. Make sure to have your hand touching your leg so that you give the treat nice and close. This trains your dog to stay very close to you.

Hide and Seek

This is an awesome game to build your dog's love of coming to you when he is called, with the added benefit of exercising his nose.It is also an ideal game during rainy days. Start by hiding behind a door or in another room. It should be easy for your dog to find you, which is the point. You want your dog to understand what game he is playing.

After hiding, call your dog. When he eventually finds you, give him a reward with treats or toys. If he is really struggling to find you, call him again, but do not make noises continuously. Doing so will only train his ear, not his nose.

As your dog becomes more proficient, you can increase the difficulty of where you hide in the house. You can start to play this game outside eventually when your dog gets better at the game. It is also a really fun way to build up speed and joy when you call your dog to you. In the future, you and your dog will be playing this game whenever you call for him.

Chapter 11: Why Relationship is Crucial

Ethologists, who are scientists that study natural animal behavior, have discovered exciting things about the emotional side of animals. This shows that dogs do not rely on their instincts alone. They have feelings just like you.

Relationship-based dog training works on the principle of addressing the needs of both the human and the dog. There will be times when dog training does not take the dog's desires into consideration. For instance, your dog may want to chase the squirrel across the street, but you do not allow him to for his own safety. However, just because he cannot do that does not mean that he feels bad because of it. We can focus on training him in a way that makes him happy.

Setting the Dog Up to Succeed

Relationship-based training is more about teaching than training. It is very similar to raising children. The education system sets children up to success. At first, they learn to count, then how to add and subtract, then multiplication and division, then the dreaded algebra. If a child has problems with any of the steps, he needs to remain in that stage until he is good enough to proceed. It is unfair to let him move up and be left in the dust because later stages of education require full knowledge of all previous stages.

The same also applies to your dog. We expect our dogs to be able to sit in the middle of a park with screaming children and naughty squirrels way before he is comfortable sitting in your quiet home. That is not such a realistic expectation, is it? If we continue to do that, we are setting our dog up for failure. It is similar to asking your kids to perform algorithmic applications before they can count above 10.

So, the idea is that we need to create an education system for our dogs as well. Start with something simple and easy. When your dog masters that step, you can then build on that success and introduce slightly challenging tasks for him to learn. Just like children, dogs can and will fail at some point during their education, and they will continue to do so much more frequently than children. This is totally fine because they just need to repeat the task until they master it before moving on. It is overly optimistic to assume that he can perform a complicated task such as bringing his toy to you when he does not even master fetch.

Follow this Formula

There are many approaches to relationship-based training, but all of them follow the same concepts. Follow this formula to set your dog up for success:

1. Teach your dog behaviors in a distraction-free environment.
2. Gradually increase the difficulty such as longer sits or stays.

3. Gradually add in distractions. Start with minor distractions then work your way up slowly.

4. Combine difficulty and distractions.

5. Do not move to the next step until the last step has been mastered.

6. If your dog has problems with any of the steps, go back to the previous step. He may not have mastered the behavior in that scenario.

7. Be clear and consistent with your instructions, including pitch, tone, and gesture.

8. Constant feedback: Make sure your dog knows that he is doing it right or wrong.

9. Pay extra attention to your dog's body language. This is your dog's means of communication. If he is stressed during the training sessions, change up the approach or end the session immediately and try again when he is more relaxed.

10. Make learning fun for both of you.

Understanding Dogs

There is a major assumption dog owners make when their dogs fail to respond to a command. They assume that their dogs know exactly what their owners want, and are just being stubborn. As a result, some owners become upset or frustrated. What we fail to consider is that our dog may have a very good reason as to why he does not want to follow our command. Consider the following:

- He may not understand the command: Dogs cannot generalize like us. They may sit when you give the command in your room, standing only feet away from them. But that does not mean that they can sit when they are in the dog park, and you are standing 10 feet away. As a general rule, it can take between 30 to 75 correct repetitions for your dog to truly understand the command. This requires consistency, as I have mentioned earlier. Incorrect repetitions do not count. So, practice the command in different but controlled situations, so your dog really understands what he needs to do.

- He may be distracted and has yet to learn how to think through distractions: This could be a case of sensory overload in which the dog's brain is so stimulated that he cannot focus. Just about anything is exciting to your dog, from a squirrel to a butterfly. Unless your dog has enough practice, he cannot think about anything else, especially the training at hand.

- He may be hurt or sick: Your dog may not be able to follow through with your command simply because he is hurt or sick. This is why it is important that you take note of how he usually behaves in any given situation. If he starts to act differently, there may be something wrong. So, learn your dog's personality quirks and pay a visit to the vet if he is behaving differently.

- Stress: Your dog may experience excessive stress, or he may be too scared to follow through with your command. Stress can result in two things: overdrive or complete shutdown. Whatever the case may be, your dog will not be able to focus on your command if he is too stressed or anxious. We have all experienced the same behavioral problem, especially during a particularly difficult exam. We tend to grind to a halt and cannot think properly. There are two ways to address this problem. First, if it is a training session, then stop the training immediately. If it is an everyday situation that is inevitable, try to make it as relaxing and not as stressful as possible. Other than that, do not ask your dog to do more than he can.

- Your dog did not hear you: This is especially prevalent in noisy or busy areas. Again, we have experienced such a problem personally. Have you ever been so absorbed in doing something that you fail to notice someone standing right behind you? If your dog is super focused on something, he is very likely to not hear what you say. Therefore, try to gain your dog's attention before you give him a command.

- Your command is not a choice: In some cases, your dog thinks that he has no reason to do what you ask. This is especially true if he is enjoying himself and then you ask him to do something. He needs a really good reason to stop having fun and do what you ask. To address this problem, work on your leadership exercises. This means you need to be clear, consistent, firm, and fair for your dog training. Help if you need to. Give your command only once and follow through as you normally would.

Conclusion

In the end, dog training does not have to be a tedious activity. Your dog learns much faster when you incorporate fun activities into the training sessions. In the end, you will have a well-behaved dog that you can take everywhere, and the bond between you two will be very strong.

In this book, we have discussed many important behaviors your dog needs to live inside your house without causing so much trouble. The only way to effectively teach your dog such behaviors is through positive reinforcement training on crate training, house training, and fundamental commands. Generally, you do not need to use clicker training unless you have been unsuccessful in your training sessions.

As mentioned earlier, there are many training methods, and they are effective in different situations. However, for dog owners at home, positive reinforcement is the best way to train your dog because it creates a positive experience for your dog without traumatizing or hurting him physically. As for the form of punishment in the context of positive training, a firm "no" or not rewarding your dog in the form of denying him attention or treats is the only means of punishment. Under any circumstances, do NOT hit, shout, or make loud noises at your dog as it will scare him and possibly render your training for naught.

By using positive reinforcement training, you can teach your dog many behaviors such as crate training by getting him to associate the crate as his private den. He should see it as a place where he can get some privacy and where he can seek safety. As mentioned previously, the best option for an in-house crate is a metal crate as you can be flexible with the size, not to mention the extra ventilation and visibility in and out of the crate. Make sure to have a plastic crate handy when you need to transport your dog around, just in case he makes a fuss. Although, if your dog is trained well, he should not do that when you let him have his own seat inside your car.

House training is just as crucial if your dog lives inside (and he should) your house. The idea is to tell him where his bathroom is when he needs to do his business. The start of the training will be slow and possibly tedious. However, with time and patience, your dog should learn where his usual spot is and will go there consistently on his own. The time and effort put into house training will be well worth it. Just make sure you recognize how your dog tells you when he needs to go.

As for the commands, there are tens of them out there that are considered important for your dog. I have highlighted a few of them because I believe they serve as a foundation upon which to train additional commands. When your dog becomes proficient with these five commands, you should be able to teach other commands relatively easily.

As you may have noticed by now, all the training I have provided above follows a certain pattern: consistency. If there is only one thing you can take away from this book, it is this one. Many times, inexperienced dog owners are inconsistent with their training system and often confuse their dogs. This leads to inefficient training and frustrated owners. So, the key again is to notice all the little details about how you teach your dog. If you use a verbal cue, make sure you say the exact same thing every time (including pitch and pace). Inconsistency in how you voice your command is one reason why dogs do not obey commands. They understand the word we speak in a certain way, but not the other.

With all that said and done, I would like to thank you for reading this far. You deserve to treat yourself for putting so much time and effort into learning how to train your dog. This is actually the first step in effective in-home dog training. The owners themselves need to know the basics, and they need to have the willingness to invest the time and effort (possibly frustration) into the training. I'm not going to lie to you. Dog training can take a long time because dogs do not learn as quickly as puppies, but that does not mean it will take forever. In the end, all of your efforts will be worth it, and you will have a well-behaved dog.

Other than that, I have one final message for you. Positive reinforcement training, which is the entirety of this book, is built on compassion for animals. I love animals, especially dogs. This is why I decided to become a dog trainer. Many dogs out there are fortunate enough to have considerate owners, but not all of them. Some dogs become victims of events ranging from being abandoned just because they are no longer cute to outright upsetting abusive behavior from their previous owners. I firmly believe that every dog is a good boy, and deserves a place to call his true home. He needs a human family. To you, a dog may be a companion for ten years or so. To him, you are his entire life. The animal shelter can only provide the bare minimum for dogs to live in. It is up to us to provide them with a home they truly deserve. It is cool to have an expensive, purebred dog at home, but when you get a dog from the shelter, you are doing everyone a favor by saving him from a harsh life and giving him a true home. Let's be honest here. Any dog is a good boy, regardless of their breed or size. With some training, time, patience, and consistency, you can effectively teach your dog all the right behaviors.

Resources

If you are interested in learning more about dog training, I have compiled a list of links you can follow:

Chapter 1

- Dog Training Methods Explained. (n.d.). Retrieved from https://www.dog-training-excellence.com/dog-training-methods.html
- 7 Most Popular Dog Training Methods - Dogtime. (2019, January 11). Retrieved from https://dogtime.com/reference/dog-training/50743-7-popular-dog-training-methods
- Dog Training: Positive Reinforcement vs. Alpha Dog Methods. (2010, October 14). Retrieved from https://pets.webmd.com/dogs/features/dog-training-positive-reinforcement-alpha-dog-method

Chapter 2

- How Do You Prepare To Bring A New Dog Home? (2019, June 12). Retrieved from https://barkpost.com/life/prepare-home-for-dog/
- Choosing the right dog. (n.d.). Retrieved from https://www.bluecross.org.uk/pet-advice/choosing-the-right-dog
- How to Choose the Dog That's Right for You. (2018, December 14). Retrieved from https://www.thesprucepets.com/how-to-choose-the-right-dog-1117320

Chapter 3

- What is Positive Reinforcement Dog Training? (n.d.). Retrieved from https://www.dogstrustdogschool.org.uk/training/i-want-to-train-my-dog/the-benefits-of-positive-reinforcement/
- 10 Best Training Tips. (2016, October 19). Retrieved from https://www.pedigree.com/dog-care/training/10-best-training-tips
- How to Train Your Dog & Top Training Tips | RSPCA. (n.d.). Retrieved from https://www.rspca.org.uk/adviceandwelfare/pets/dogs/training

Chapter 4

- Housebreak a Dog with Positive Reinforcement. (2019, May 2). Retrieved from https://www.wikihow.com/Housebreak-a-Dog-with-Positive-Reinforcement
- Crate Training. (n.d.). Retrieved from https://positively.com/dog-behavior/puppy-knowledge/puppy-housetraining/crate-training/

- How To Get Your Dog To Enjoy The Crate. (n.d.). Retrieved from https://positively.com/dog-behavior/basic-cues/how-to-get-your-dog-to-enjoy-the-crate/

Chapter 5

- Admin. (2019, June 13). Tips for Potty Training Your New Puppy | Hill's Pet. Retrieved from https://www.hillspet.com/dog-care/training/puppy-potty-training-tips
- Tips for Housetraining Your Puppy. (2009, December 16). Retrieved from https://pets.webmd.com/dogs/guide/house-training-your-puppy#1

Chapter 6

- Basic Dog Training Commands. (n.d.). Retrieved from https://www.purina.co.uk/dogs/behaviour-and-training/training-your-dog/basic-commands-for-your-dog
- 3 ways positive reinforcement can change your pet's behaviour. (n.d.). Retrieved from https://www.petplan.co.uk/pet-information/dog/advice/positive-reinforcement-dog-behaviour-training/
- How to Train a Dog to Sit Using Positive Reinforcement. (n.d.). Retrieved from https://www.embracepetinsurance.com/waterbowl/article/how-to-train-a-dog-to-sit

Chapter 7

- Dog training equipment and supplies for positive reinforcement dog training from North Coast pets. (n.d.). Retrieved from https://www.northcoastpets.com/Dog-Training-Equipment-s/156.htm
- Training Equipment. (n.d.). Retrieved from https://positively.com/dog-training/methods-equipment/training-equipment/

Chapter 8

- Clicker Training. (n.d.). Retrieved from https://positively.com/dog-training/methods-equipment/training-methods/clicker-training/

Chapter 9

- How to Handle 6 Common Dog Behavior Problems. (2013, November 13). Retrieved from https://www.petcarerx.com/article/how-to-handle-6-common-dog-behavior-problems/1461
- Dog Behavior. (n.d.). Retrieved from https://positively.com/dog-behavior/

Chapter 10

- 13 Dog Training Games and Exercises with Video Demos | Journey Dog Training. (2019, June 7). Retrieved from https://journeydogtraining.com/13-dog-training-games/

Chapter 11

- 13 Dog Training Games and Exercises with Video Demos | Journey Dog Training. (2019, June 7). Retrieved from https://journeydogtraining.com/13-dog-training-games/
- Relationship-Based Dog Training Philosophy | Lincoln Dog Trainers. (n.d.). Retrieved from https://inrelationwithdogs.com/dog-training-philosophy/

CPSIA information can be obtained
at www.ICGtesting.com
Printed in the USA
BVHW010556080620
580993BV00010B/893

9 781989 638408